THE BACK TO BASICS
BOOK OF MONEY!

A Couple's Guide to Financial Peace

ISBN: 1-4392-2777-2

BOOKS BY JOHN R. INGRISANO

The Insurance Dictionary

The Back to Basics Book of Selling!
A Guide To A Successful Sales Career
(www.TheFreestyleEntrepreneur.com)

A Perfect Day
Thoughts on Faith & Forgiveness
(www.DailyConnections.net)

The Back to Basics Book of Money!
A Couple's Guide to Financial Peace
(www.b2bbook ofmoney.com)

The Back to Basics Book of Money!

A Couple's Guide to Financial Peace

By
John R. Ingrisano

John R. Ingrisano
Custom Communications
204 Lakeview Drive
Algoma, WI 54201
(920) 559-3722
john@b2bbookofmoney.com

For more information on money
management skills, visit:
www.b2bbookofmoney.com

Cover Design by April A. Adams
www.AdamsAdmin.com

DEDICATION

To my children – Jon, Nicky and Angie –
who make everything worth the price.

About the Author

John R. Ingrisano has been writing and teaching about money matters and business management for more than 30 years. An educator, communicator, sales trainer and marketing strategist, he enjoys working with clients that range in size from huge, multi-national financial corporations to Mom 'n Pop shops across Main Street, USA.

He is the author of four books and thousands of articles, a business journalist and columnist, and a classroom instructor on subjects ranging from leadership communications to money management.

Group and financial wellness seminars include such topics as …

- Husbands, Wives & Money
- How to Get Out of Debt
- How to Spend Money (Intelligently)
- Teens & Money
- How to Make Money
- How to Live Well on What You Earn

Table of Contents

Money Doesn't Just Talk. It Screams!

My friend John R. Ingrisano, author of this excellent book, and I were attending a performance recently of "Fiddler on the Roof." Prior to the show, we were talking about how it amazed us that our kids could be grown and now having kids of their own. Time had moved quickly, in retrospect. Life was good for us. We had gone through graduate school, had authored books, had bought nice homes, had gotten our kids reared and even through college, and we were both still in good health. Yep, life was good.

As we watched the musical, the main character, Tevye, began to sing a song of lament called, "If I Was a Rich Man." In the song he speculated as to how his life could be so much better if he could just be a man of wealth – he would have a fine home with nice staircases; he would have servants his wife could order around; he would have time to read and study; and, best of all, right or wrong, people would revere his thoughts, ideas and advice. In short, being rich was a whole lot better than being poor.

One of the reasons that "Fiddler" is still being watched and talked about is because it contains solid wisdom like that. Tevye was right. It's no fun being poor. In fact, it's no fun not even living up to the full financial potential we each have.

America is a land of polemic contrasts. It contains the wealthiest people on the planet, as well as the most destitute. How can such a dichotomy be true, especially if this is a land of free enterprise, genuine capitalism, and endless opportunity? The answer is found in one word: *savvy*. When it comes to money management, some folks have it, others don't.

John Ingrisano is savvy. He knows about investing, portfolio building, reducing debt, setting and reaching monetary goals, spending wisely, and finding financial comfort. For more than three decades John has dispersed this information as a book author, newsletter writer and editor, and magazine and newspaper columnist. Additionally, he has developed training films, spoken at universities, and taught seminars at business conventions and conferences. John reads and probes and studies and examines and analyzes anything related to the field of money management. His insights are based on experience but are honed by cutting edge current data. In short, John knows his stuff.

If you get a chance to hear John speak sometime, don't miss it. Meanwhile, the book you are holding is "the goods" in regard to providing solid tips and guidelines for bringing your finances into line. You'll "hear" John's voice as you read the lessons found herein. Sometimes he'll encourage you; sometimes he'll admonish you; sometimes he'll coach you; but at all times he'll teach you.

Tevye desired to be a "rich man." John Ingrisano desires for you to have a *rich life*. Indeed, finances are a large part of that. But so are your peace of mind, personal security, feelings of self-fulfillment, and optimism regarding the future. You'll find the paths to each of these aspects of the rich life herein. Take the first step: turn to Chapter One.

Dennis E. Hensley, Ph.D.
Author of *Money Wise* and
How to Manage Your Money

Introduction
The Challenge of Money

> *"With all thy getting,*
> *get thee understanding."*
> **—Proverbs 4:7**

You're Here Because....

Okay, it isn't that you don't know how to work. And it isn't that you aren't being paid pretty well. You probably are. The thing that is bugging you is that you're still broke, running along on a work-and-spend financial treadmill. And it's getting old ... very old.

So, why are you here? What are *you* looking for? You have opened this book for a reason. Perhaps you, too, are fed up with worrying about money. Perhaps you are tired of running ever faster on a seemingly endless financial treadmill that has you working and spending and never getting ahead. You are here because you want to change something in your life. Perhaps you have a serious financial problem. Perhaps the only meaningful conversation you and your partner have these days is an ongoing "discussion" about money ... and it's starting to take a big toll on your relationship. Or perhaps you just want to get more bang for the bucks you earn and spend. For whatever reason you are here, you want to find a better way.

You probably know people who seem to have found that better way. They are most likely no brighter or better than you. Maybe they are even earning less money than you. However, they are the ones with the nicer home, the newer car, more cash in their pockets and more upscale clothes on their backs. They have the time and the money to take a cruise in the winter and loaf around the pool (oh, yes, they have a pool, too) in the summer. They are the ones with an ever-fattening piggy bank to pay for their children's college educations and an ever-expanding retirement portfolio to assure their own financial independence by the time they hit age 62. "He can't be making that much money," you tell yourself, or wonder, "How can she afford that jewelry?"

Most of all, they seem happy! They seem to get along. They seem satisfied with each other and in harmony with the universe.

Assuming they are not living beyond their means on borrowed money and borrowed time, and they haven't inherited a huge chunk of change from a rich uncle, they might know something you don't. It just might be that they have mastered the art and science – the critical skills – of how to take full control of their financial destiny. It is very likely that they understand money. They know how to manage it. They know how to harness and use it to achieve their goals. They know how to put it to work to build the lifestyle they want.

Good for them. And good for you, too, because there is nothing they have done that you cannot do, too... maybe even better than they are doing it.

$ $ $

How to Get the Most from This Book

Travel through it at your own pace. You will learn 10 valuable money skills. You and your partner may want to tackle one each week. Think about each skill and how to master it.

Each chapter refers to several assignments, called Wealth Builders. These are contained in the *Back to Basics Book of Money Workbook.* The workbook will help you take the ideas you learn here and apply them to your life. That is because reading a book about money management will not make your financially stable. However, putting the ideas into action will.

Make sure you have the workbook with you when you begin. Then be sure to take the time to complete each Wealth Builder assignment before going on to the next skill. After that, be sure to practice, refine and expand on what you learn in each chapter. As you apply the concepts, you will begin to feel the impact of financial peace and growing prosperity almost immediately.

$ $ $

Got Money Troubles? Join the Club!

> *"Knowledge is power.*
> *Knowledge in action is success."*
>
> **—Source Unknown**

One of my favorite commercials on television features a nicely dressed suburbanite. He has a silly grin plastered on his face as he talks about the good life he is enjoying. We see him mowing his neatly trimmed lawn while sitting on his expensive rider mower; cleaning the pool in his backyard; and teeing off on the golf course at the country club with his friends. "How do I do it?" he asks the camera. "I'm in debt up to my eyeballs," he says, still smiling, and then adds, "I can barely make my minimum monthly payments. Somebody help me."

$ $ $

A Nation Up to Its Eyeballs …

The frightening part about that commercial is that it contains more truth than a number of couples want to acknowledge. While many of us live well, few of us are truly well off. We drive cars purchased with auto loans that we never quite pay off before trading them in for newer models. Or we just lease them, which guarantees perpetual payments. We buy homes with minimum money down, take out 30-year mortgages, and then borrow out any appreciation with home equity loans. We go on cruises we cannot afford and pay for them with credit cards that charge us as much as 18 to 21 percent interest. We buy furniture on installment and willingly pay 25 percent on each dollar borrowed. And … well, you get the picture.

In the United States of America – a country that, in spite of recent economic setbacks, is still the wealthiest country on earth – the majority of households, whether earning annual incomes of $30,000 or $300,000, live from paycheck to paycheck, teetering on the brink of financial disaster. Part of it has to do with how much we save ... or don't save. In 1985, Americans put aside 11 percent of their incomes. That was our high water mark as a nation, and it's been downhill ever since. By the close of the last century, we were still managing to save two or three percent of our incomes each year. However, in 2005, according to U.S. Department of Commerce figures, something frightening and weird happened. We not only quit saving, but we started dipping into what we had already squirreled away. As of the writing of this book, we are showing signs of stopping what is called "negative saving," but the rate we put aside still limps along at around one percent, not a terrific showing.[1]

At first glance, we appear to be doing fairly well. After all, the median net worth for all Americans hovered right around $90,000 to $100,000 in 2004.[2] Unfortunately, for homeowners, much of that wealth came from market appreciation of their houses. I say "unfortunately" because when that housing bubble burst in 2008, along with it went billions of dollars in wealth. However, in reality, it was mostly wealth "on paper."

Then there are the nearly 31 percent of U.S. households that have a net worth below $25,000 (and that includes everything from their cars and boats to furniture and television sets), and 11 percent who have negative net worth; they owe more than they own.

Still, the real problem is that many of us are way over our heads in debt, paying huge chunks of money in interest on credit cards and other easy-pay installment loans – very often to buy things that we really don't need, really don't want, and really can't afford. As a result, according to the credit bureau Experian, the average American with a credit file is responsible for $16,635 in debt, excluding mortgages.[3] At even a low interest rate (by

---

[1] "Personal Saving Rate," U.S. Department of Commerce, December 23, 2008.
[2] "How Much Are You Worth?" CNNMoney.com (August 20, 2004)
[3] "The End of Credit Card Consumerism," *U.S. News and World Report*, August 2008

credit card standards) of 10 percent, that comes out to $1,663.50 a year (nearly $140 per month) in interest payments alone. At 18 percent interest, the amount of interest paid comes to nearly $3,000 a year, or more than $250 a month in interest charges alone! And that's not just for one year. Many of us carry maximum debt loads while making minimum payments year after year after year … and think nothing of it.

I knew a fellow years ago who, when I proudly told him that I had just made my last payment on my car, wanted to know what car I was going to buy now. He was horrified when I told him I was going to drive my debt-free vehicle for a few more years. He actually told me that I was wasting all that available credit by not using it!

This fellow was a good example of how lack of money is not the problem. The real culprit is a lack of understanding how to use money most effectively. Many couples bring good incomes in the front door and then let that money slip out the back door without even noticing by wasteful spending. Once again, the problem generally has little to do with how much money they make. That is only part of the financial equation. It is not necessarily how much they earn, but how they manage their money, that counts. (Remember, if you bring home $100,000 a year and spend $101,000, you are financially worse off than if you earn $35,000 and spend $34,999.)

If this describes your life today, the good news is that you do not have to continue living this way, always teetering on the brink of financial chaos. It is possible to live well on what you earn, to stop shelling out your hard-earned money to everyone else, and to start building a rock-solid lifestyle and financial security for yourself and your family.

In short, it is possible – and not all that difficult – to achieve financial peace.

$$$

Many of Us Are a Paycheck Away from Disaster

- *The savings rate for Americans is the lowest it has been in 73 years. (Parade Magazine, April 23, 2006.)*

- *One-third of Americans have no retirement savings and most are not eligible for a pension. (Social Security Administration Basic Facts, July 2004)*

- *Seventy-two percent of Americans don't have enough savings to meet short-term emergencies. (National Investment Watch Survey, A.G. Edwards Inc., 2004)*

- *One in six families with credit cards pays only the minimum due every month. (Source: Experian National Score Index Study, February 2007)*

- *Twenty-eight percent of those surveyed say their ability to pay off their credit card balance has become more difficult. (Source: Javelin Strategy & Research, "Credit Card Issuer Profitability in a Difficult Economy," July 2008)*

Three Facts About Money

I have always found money interesting and challenging. I have written about and taught money management skills for 30 years. Three major things I have learned about people and money during those three decades:

#1: Most People Struggle with Money

First, as I mentioned above, many people struggle when it comes to using money as an effective tool to achieve their goals. (For that matter, many people have no goals. They just earn and spend in a relentless cycle.) This is mostly because they have not given much thought to money, except to spend it and then worry about it on a daily basis. In fact, to be painfully blunt, there are those among us who are flat-out ignorant when it comes to money. I have met people over the years who see no connection between the income they earn and the lifestyle they live. That is not meant to be a blame or judgment statement, just a fact. They do not have a clue how to use money, manage money, do much more than work like dogs 40 or more hours a week to earn money, and then turn around and spend it like drunken sailors on shore leave. They earn it and spend it and borrow it. The bank and the credit card companies – everyone but themselves – are in control of their financial lives.

#2: Money Problems Can Destroy Relationships

Second, while money cannot make people happy, the lack – or mismanagement – of money can make them miserable. Because of their financial situation, many couples find that their lives are out of balance, if not completely out of control, not just financially but in every respect. Keep in mind that there is a close correlation between money problems and domestic problems. Look at most divorces. When we get beyond "He's a jerk," and "She's impossible to please," the real reason behind most divorces and marital problems is MONEY. Worry over money can eat away at couples in subtle ways, producing terrible stress that can tear families apart.

Financial problems are almost always part of the mix – in there somewhere – when it comes to divorce and marital discord. Studies differ as to whether money comes in first, second or third (competing with sex and how to rear children as the top argument topics), but it seems to be always present in some form. One study found that money was a source of tension between 84 percent of couples, with the number one cause of dissension being priorities about how to manage or allocate money.[4] Another showed that 70 percent of couples have the "money talk" at least once a week ("Honey, we have to cut back

---

[4] "Marriage and Money," *Money* on CNN.com (March 2006)

somewhere." "Okay, let's go out for pizza and talk about it.") and that 40 percent say they have lied about how much they spent on an item they recently purchased.[5] One thing is certain: money is the most common reason for arguments, what couples fight about the most, and the number one reason divorcing couples *say* is the cause.

As the Money Went, So Went the Marriage

Steve and Cathy had been married for 22 years. They were as happy as most people. He was a businessman; and she was a teacher. He had always done well, until he got involved in a business venture that proved to be the wrong idea at the wrong time.

As the situation deteriorated and the gauge on the bank account slid steadily toward EMPTY, so did their relationship. Their financial struggles took a terrible toll on an otherwise happy and stable marriage.

As Cathy became needy and insecure, Steve became withdrawn, consumed by the business and the growing red ink puddling around the bottom line. They found themselves engaged in discussions (i.e. arguments) that had nothing to do with money: he wasn't listening; she was nagging; he griped about the leaky bathroom faucet (perhaps subconsciously comparing it to their resources, which were steadily dripping away); she expressed concern about how he was becoming irritable and forgetting things, such as their anniversary.

And on it went. The business failed. So did the marriage. The cause: money woes!

---

[5] "Love & Money," *SmartMoney*, February 9, 2004.

On the other hand, money can be an amazing source of marital harmony and unity. When finances are in balance, when couples are in agreement and pulling together in unison, this common cause serves to strengthen the bonds of the relationship. At the very least, it provides a stable platform upon which to build harmony and settle other differences. Perhaps that's because being financially in control and secure makes people happier and more confident. Take away ongoing money concerns and most folks would walk through their days with heads held higher. They'd sleep a lot better, too.

I'm not a psychologist, but I do know that when I'm not worried about money, I enjoy every other aspect of life more fully, and I'm much more pleasant to be around. I suspect you are the same. If you doubt it, ask yourself how worrying about paying an overdue bill, using a credit card when you know you are already having trouble making payments, or finding that you have a 31-day month but only a 28-day paycheck – how all these distract you and reduce your ability to enjoy life.

In that same vein, did you ever notice that you often can spot people who have money in the bank? We sometimes see them as having arrogant attitudes, but the fact is that (for many, at least) they simply have a quiet calm about them. They seem more relaxed than those of us who are wondering about how to pay next month's mortgage or pulling out the sofa cushions looking for change to pay the pizza delivery guy. Money makes a difference in our attitudes and our confidence. It is a powerful tool.

#3: Financial Health & Stability Can Start TODAY!

Finally, I learned that no matter how bad a person's financial situation may be, it is NEVER hopeless. It can be turned around and fixed. Depending on how deep the hole, it may take time to crawl out of it, but every day can show some improvement in standard of living.

No, the cure is not always easy and can rarely be completed in a flash, but if you are determined to improve the quality of your life and your relationship, you can start today, and you will be amazed at the positive changes that will begin almost immediately to flow into your life. Most of all, every day that your finances can be improved by a fraction, an inch, and then a foot (or perhaps better stated as a penny, a nickel, and then a dime), brings you that much closer to financial security, strength and peace.

What is the alternative? Ignoring financial problems is like speeding a hundred miles an hour down a highway with a brick wall around a bend. You may not know which bend, but that wall is there, and the crash will be a messy one. Guaranteed. So, the time is now to slow it down, turn it around and head in the opposite direction.

You are reading this book because you and your partner are struggling with money matters. The good news is that you are aware of the problem, and a problem identified is a problem already half solved. This book will give you a roadmap and the tools you need to do the job and help you turn around your financial condition and the overall quality of your life.

$ $ $

The Bottom Line About The Bottom Line

The fundamentals of money management are simple, easy to understand and easy to apply. All you need is determination, self-discipline, and the ideas in this book. You can start up the road to financial well-being (and a happier, more satisfying personal life) almost immediately, whether your financial situation today is just a bit out of whack or careening wildly out of control.

Young & Relentless

Andrea was like some of the millions of young people who struggled with money. Nobody had bothered to teach her money management basics or the big difference between lifestyle (all the trappings of a good life) and standard of living (ability to afford the good life). At 24, on her own, she was living the good life, with a comfortable apartment, nice car, and many of the other outward signs of a successful life. It was a great lifestyle. The only problem was that she was living way, way beyond her means. Spending about 25 percent more each month than she was earning (the clerks in the mall stores knew her by name), she was skittering wildly down a slippery slope, on a merry sleigh ride down the hill into financial disaster.

Finally, her finances deteriorated to the point that she could no longer ignore the situation. She became moody and depressed, walking around with a dark cloud over her head. She kept saying how she needed more money, even while continuing to max out her credit cards and spend money randomly and without priority. When she finally hit bottom, she was four months behind on her car payments and two months late on her rent, with no phone and more than $12,000 in credit card debt. She was also paying (or at least accumulating) $180 a month, more than $2,160 a year, in interest on those credit cards!

Finally, one day, it dawned on her. She had to make a change, a big change. She took drastic measures: she set a goal and mapped out a strategy to claw her way out of the financial pit she had dug for herself, and to do it in two years, just 24 months. She moved to a much smaller apartment, traded down her car for one more affordable, contacted all her creditors and worked out payment schedules, put away all her credit cards, and began living frugally.

She missed her goal by six months. It took her two and a half years, but she did it. Today she drives a nice car, but it is one that she can afford, and she lives comfortably. She can even afford a reasonable vacation each year, which she pays for in cash from money she saves. No, it was not easy. Her case was extreme, and she had to overhaul her entire lifestyle. But the personal payback was incredible.

Best of all, her growing knowledge and money management skill have done wonders for her self-esteem. She no longer uses shopping as a kind of "comfort food" or ignores bills that once piled up in a corner on the kitchen counter. She lives frugally, sleeps better at night, and actually enjoys living on a cash basis, with her credit cards held in reserve for emergencies only. She even gets a kick out of the "game" of money management: clipping coupons, taking pride in shopping for sales, deciding sometimes to tell herself "no" when an expenditure would not fit into her spending plan.

========

The ideas in this book can help you get your finances and your life under control. Learn and master the 10 Couples Money Skills and every week your finances will begin to grow healthier and stronger. In the sections that follow, you will learn the importance of money and how to use it wisely to achieve your goals and live better. You will learn universal principles about money that work. Without understanding and applying these principles, you could pick up a windfall of $1,000,000 and, like many young sports superstars, end up dead broke. (I have seen it happen, as people I have known went through a half-million dollar inheritance in two years.) Armed with knowledge about these principles, however, you can discover how to live – well and happily – on what you earn, whether your income is $500,000 a year or $25,000!

Your knowledge and money management mastery will grow steadily with each page. In just several months, you can be on solid financial ground, enjoying all the financial and relationship benefits of your efforts. It will require some time, discipline and dedication. However, the rewards will far outstrip the effort that is required. By learning and applying the basic principles in this book, which will help you master simple money management techniques, you can boost your quality of life and standard of living by getting more value for your money. And as I said earlier, it can also improve your relationship with your spouse or significant other.

$ $ $

Wealth Builder #1
How Do You Rate As a Money Manager?

Let's figure out how you stand as a money manager. Go to *The Back to Basics Book of Money Workbook* and complete the first Wealth Builder, which is a self-quiz to help you assess your own money skills. Need a workbook? You can order your copy by going to www.b2bbookofmoney.com.

$ $ $

If you are doing a lot right, this book will show you how to tighten up your money management skills and become a master of your financial fate. If you are floundering amid a financial malaise, this book will help you get on track to financial health and get the best value for your money.

When you are ready, take a deep breath and turn the page. We'll start by examining – and very possibly realigning – your relationship with your partner, at least when it comes to money matters.

$ $ $

Couple Money Skill #1

Make Your Partner Your Financial Partner (Assemble Your "Financial Peace" Team)

> *"A house divided against itself cannot stand."*
>
> **—Abraham Lincoln**

This book is about money management for couples. So, let me begin by saying that you must – I repeat, MUST – work together to address your financial issues. One cannot do it alone. It will take both of you. If you work together, you can accomplish miracles. If one of you takes up the challenge of mastering the money skills while the other is disinterested (or perhaps even hostile to the idea), your probability of success will decrease dramatically. The key is to work together. Do this, and you financial picture will increase dramatically and quickly. Plus, you will enjoy the feeling of taking on this challenge together, as a couple and a team. Believe me, it's well worth it. So, let's go.

$ $ $

United You Stand. Divided You Fall.

You are in this together. If you have children, they are part of it too. So it is time to get your crew together. I am not talking about bankers and financial advisors, though you may need them later. This is about your family. If you are married (or have a financially involved significant other), it is critically important that you work together as a team to successfully manage your money. If you have children at the age of dissent, bring them into the discussion, if only to help them understand that some changes are in the wind.

Why? Because, as you probably realize – if you haven't already experienced it in some form – money can be a powerful weapon in relationships. When a couple is on the same track and in agreement on financial decisions, the potential for success in mastering money management is significantly improved. However, when a couple is at odds over money, the entire relationship can become a frustrating, destructive tug of war.

===

Les & Barb: Marital Guerilla Warfare

Les and Barb engaged in "marital guerilla warfare" for years. He would go to the boat show and come home with a new, $8,500 toy, without ever having discussed his decision with Barb first. She would retaliate by re-carpeting the living room ($2,700). This went on constantly.

They were in a race to the poor house. They spent their whole lives struggling to keep their heads above water. They lived from paycheck to paycheck (sometimes four or five paychecks behind), devoting much of their income to paying off installment debt (while constantly adding more) and handing over thousands of dollars each year in interest to creditors, while buying junk neither of them really wanted.

Fortunately (and no one quite knows why), they realized one day what they were doing. They sat down one evening and had an eye-opening, heart-to-heart discussion about money and their finances. Together, finally working as a team, they began to explore ways to get out of the financial pit they had dug for themselves. They both vowed to never make a major purchase without talking to each other first.

Together they pledged to stop spending and begin aggressively paying off their bills. Their story had a happy ending, as they began eliminating their debts and saving money with a vengeance. However, it was a hard-learned lesson, one that could have turned out much differently.

===

If you want to fight, throw dishes at each other. Just make sure you realize that, if you use money as a weapon, you are hurting not just the other person, but also yourself and everyone who depends on you.

Sally & Lou: Biting the Bullet Together

Sally and Lou had what could be described as a perfect relationship. He was proud of his income-earning ability, bringing home over $200,000 a year, which allowed her to buy whatever she wanted. They both liked the situation. He earned and she spent, and it did seem like they had a perfect, symbiotic relationship. Then one day it came time to talk about retirement. It turned out that their home, which they had purchased 25 years ago, had almost no equity. Over the years, they had refinanced their house time and time again, pulling out its increased appreciated value to support an extravagant lifestyle. As it turned out, in spite of Lou's excellent income, they had been living just a tad above their means all this time. Having earned millions of dollars over the last several decades, they were essentially flat broke!

In a blinding flash of recognition, Lou realized that he had worked all those years, earning an excellent income, but they would not be able to retire! He would need to work until the day he died. Sally had no idea that they were living from paycheck to paycheck. She assumed that their finances were as solid as the Rock of Gibraltar. Their biggest problem was lack of communication. They both had assumed that everything was on track and financially fine. They thought that their strong income and their affluent lifestyle were proof that they were financially healthy.

Finally, they sat down and talked. Together, finally working as a team, they began to explore ways to get out of the financial pit they had dug for themselves. She volunteered to cut up her credit cards; he vowed to be more communicative about their finances and to keep working ten more years; together they

25

pledged to stop spending and begin aggressively socking away money for the future – more than $100,000 a year.

When they told a friend this story, he said to them, "Congratulations, you two, your partner of 30 years has now become your financial partner."

====

Charlie & Rose: On the Same Page from the Start

Charlie and Rose just celebrated their 35th wedding anniversary. They started out together with a keen, almost instinctive sense of money management. Neither earned much during their salad days. That did not matter. They were frugal and always lived within their means. Except for a mortgage, they carried zero debt. Together they set up a household budget, paid their bills together, and discussed every major (and many minor) financial decision. Plus, from their early days, they put aside five percent of everything they earned. Eventually, they increased that amount to 10 percent.

As a result, their wealth grew, gradually at first, then a little faster and finally by leaps and bounds in the decades that followed. While many of their friends enjoyed lavish vacations and purchased new cars every two years, Charlie and Rose lived conservatively, though comfortably, never doing without what they needed, but not wasting money either. They put their children through college, lived in a nice home, and drove nice cars (Fords and Toyotas mostly, not Cadillacs or Lexuses). They worked together to acquire all the things they needed and many of the things they simply wanted. They did it by pulling together as a team and making sure they received the very best value for the money they spent, never wasting money on stuff that promised to turn into little more than minimum-value expenses.

The punch line: while many of their friends were still on the earn-and-spend treadmill, Charlie and Rose retired at age 55 … free of financial concerns. Their mortgage had been paid off, and their net worth topped seven figures. Best of all, their marriage was strong, their bankbook was solid, and their life together was in complete balance. They could not have done it without each other.

The point of these stories is to show how couples can work together and recognize that mutual money management and cooperation is the key to financial stability. This is why you must work together to build financial stability, because this teamwork can have a positive impact on your relationship and everything you do together.

$$$

Wealth Builder #2
Working as a Team

Now it's time to make a commitment to yourselves and to each other to work together to learn and master the principles in this book. Go to The *Back to Basics Book of Money Workbook*, and complete the Wealth Builder project #2, Working as a Team.

$$$

Do You Engage in "Marital Guerilla Warfare"?

In case you do not already know it, be aware that couples and money can be a unique and strange combination. The working relationship between couples can be the cornerstone of domestic hell or household heaven! When couples are not on the same page – perhaps she likes to stash the cash, he likes to flash it – the result is not a home, but a battleground, a constant tug of war, with no winners.

This can be a common problem even in the best of relationships. You can be a loving, caring couple and still be pulling in different directions in terms of how you view and manage money. The result can be that spare change falls out of your pockets and through the cracks of your life together by the bucketful. And it can add up quickly.

We will not go into the psychology of marital guerilla warfare, but here are some of its more insidious symptoms and battle tactics:

- In some relationships, one doles out and controls the money, making the other feel dependent. As a result, money is positioned as a power weapon. This is not to say that one person cannot handle all the day-to-day money management in your relationship, or even take the lead in initiating major decisions. However, unless there is good communication and agreement between both of you, this approach can be extremely destructive in the long run. It promotes secretiveness and dishonesty in money affairs and the relationship itself.

- In others, couples take a *yours-and-mine* approach to funds ... the two-paycheck dilemma. This segregation of assets is okay in theory. However, this separate approach rarely works for long in practice, especially if there are children involved or one person's assets are disproportionate to those of the other. In these situations, the *balance of power* can be difficult to maintain. That is simply because the couple is generally not working together as a ... well, as a couple. (Yes, this approach does work for some couples, especially for those who come together later in life, with established and independent assets. In these situations, each is responsible for his or her own financial management. Even so, unless both are financially responsible, there is always the risk that one person's behavior can threaten the financial well-being of the other.)

- Another destructive tactic is spite spending (as seen in our Les and Barb example), where one person spends money without discussing it first with the partner, so the other retaliates. This is really where neither controls the spending. They are like two enemies tethered together and trying to see who can hurt the other more. Over time, they can squander huge sums, wasting money on things neither one of them wants or needs. Also, the odds of the relationship lasting very long are pretty slim, since both of them live under constant pressure. In addition to learning better money management skills, they should also invest in some joint counseling.

- And then there is secret hoarding and secret spending, which generally occurs when one person earns all or a disproportionately large share of the couple's income, and the other person feels insecure and without any control. Or it can result when they have discussed money problems and one (or both) either ignores their decisions or finds that sticking to sound, cooperative money management is just too difficult.

Keep in mind that out-of-control spending, sometimes referred to as *shopaholism*, can be a very difficult habit to break. It can lead to guilt and discontent. If you are involved with a person with shopaholic tendencies (which we will discuss later), berating and nagging is not the answer. This just leads to more secret spending and a growing problem.

Secret hoarding is a sign of insecurity. Secret spending is a control problem, where one person is afraid to acknowledge his or her right to use the couple's money. Whatever the cause, such marital guerilla warfare tactics are destructive. In the end, no one wins.

Grant & Dianne: The Shopaholic

Grant and Dianne were an ambitious, hardworking young couple. Both put in long hours to buy their home and build the life they wanted. Grant thought everything was fine, until he began seeing unexpected charges on their credit card bills. When he talked about the charges to Dianne, she first denied that she had made the purchases. Later, she backtracked and apologized for spending the money.

He thought the problem was over, until six months later when he found unexplained deductions from their savings account and, following up, a separate checkbook in Dianne's name. They had long talks about money. Dianne cried and expressed remorse, with promises to stop spending money. Nothing helped. The problem grew.

Two years later, their accounts depleted, their credit in tatters, the bank demanding immediate payment for overdue mortgage bills, Dianne moved out and Grant filed for divorce. Today, he is paying off his debts and slowly rebuilding his life. He does not know where Dianne is living.

In a classic 1950s-1960s relationship, my father controlled all money issues in our household, giving my mother an "allowance" each week. She resented the situation and used to "steal" cash from his pocket when he took a shower. He retaliated by placing *his* money in a plastic bag and taking it into the shower with him. Yes, it got that silly. Whenever she got money, she would hide it. After their deaths, while going through their estates, I found several thousand dollars squirreled away in books and other places around the house. My only thought was, "That's no way to live."

$ $ $

Finding a Better Way

Horror stories behind us, let's now look at a better way: start viewing your relationship as an *economic* relationship, a personal business partnership. Remember, there is a lot more than money at stake. When you and your partner see eye-to-eye on money issues – agree on common goals, how to spend, how to save – it's not just the balance sheet that benefits. The personal relationship generally fares better, too, creating a win/win situation for everyone. You are a partnership, a team, and you need each other. Work together.

This may require a shift – some flexibility and a lot of communication. Very often, one person in the household is the financial point person. That individual pays the bills each month, hands out allowances to the children, and oversees pretty much every financial decision. By the way, that approach is neither right nor wrong. There is generally a logical reason for this one-sided division of responsibilities. Sometimes one person likes to manage the money, even enjoys it, while the other has little if any interest in these matters and does not really care about or want to know about them.

In one respect, this can be easy if your partner is agreeable and will go along with the steps the other is taking, if there is a solid foundation of trust between the couple. On the other hand, however, if one partner is both disinterested AND likes to spend money with impunity, you both have a challenge on your hands. If you are the point person (and I must assume you are also the one reading this book), you have to get your partner's attention and interest in what you are undertaking here. You have to sell your partner on the need for adjustments in your lifestyle.

You need to help your partner understand that by working together, you both can accomplish miracles with your finances and your life. It is up to both of you to educate your family and help them understand that you will all live better by working together to rein in and get control of household spending and money management habits. That can be more difficult than you think, not necessarily because your family does not care, but because most people do not understand the rules of money and the importance of taking a proactive approach to managing it.

This also applies to your children, by the way. If you have teenagers living at home, they need to be brought into the discussion. Children are expensive. Though exact figures will vary from family to family, government statistics estimate that the cost of raising one child from birth to age 18 for families making $70,200 a year averages a whopping $269,520. Higher-income families in urban areas in the West spend the most, $284,460.

Though not as steep, the figures for lower-income families are just as unsettling: $184,320 for families earning $41,700 to $70,200 and $134,370 for families making less than that.[6] Naturally, the cost increases with each child. And that does NOT factor in college educations, which averages between $26,000 (for public colleges) and $100,000 (for private universities) just for tuition and fees for four years.[7] Add another $5,000 to $10,000 a year for room, board and miscellaneous expenses. By the time you are done, the total college bill easily can run from a *low* of $50,000 to as much as $140,000 for a four-year diploma. And that's just for one child; few schools give multi-child discounts.

So, your children are a factor – a major factor – in smart money management decisions. Plus, if you have been paying for an extravagant lifestyle for your children, they may have a hard time understanding as you begin to change the household rules. "Why can't I have my own car? Tanya does?" "Why can't I go to soccer camp this year? It only costs $1,800." "Oh...My...God! Are we poor? What will my friends think if I come to school in these old rags?"

---

[6] U.S. Department of Agriculture, 2004
[7] "2008–2009 College Costs," *The College Board*, collegeboard.com, 2008

On one hand, your financial decisions are not their business. It is *your* money, after all. On the other, your financial decisions will affect them as well, making it their business, too. They are part of your household, and your decisions will directly impact them just as much – perhaps even more so – as they affect you. They can help you, or they can do everything possible to torpedo your efforts. You may be able to succeed without their cooperation. However, remember, one of your goals is to achieve and maintain domestic peace, not create a siege mentality in your own home. So, as you make changes in the weeks ahead regarding how you manage your money, they really do need to be kept informed and, in some cases, enlisted in the cause for fiscal responsibility. (Children under age 12 are not as much of a concern in these matters. Whether or not you include them is up to you. With teenagers, though, you want them on your team.)

$ $ $

Wealth Builder #3
Understanding Each Other Financially

How well do you know each other financially? To find out, complete the self-quiz exercise located in the *Back to Basics Book of Money Workbook.*

$ $ $

Wealth Builder #4
Hold a "Financial Peace" Meeting

Now, let's go to the next step, which is to share how each other feels about money and to introduce the idea of change. Working with the agenda in the *Back to Basics Book of Money Workbook*, plan and carry out a family meeting to discuss money.

$ $ $

Wealth Builder #5
Setting Mutual Goals

Where do you want to be five years from now? It's time to start thinking about how you would answer that question. Draft your financial goals using the planning section in the *Back to Basics Book of Money Workbook*.

$ $ $

What's Next: Congratulations! You should now have a growing sense of the challenges ahead of you. If you are concerned, rest assured that they are not that difficult. Take them one step and one skill at a time. Many people find that the taking up the challenge of managing money is fun. You just might, too. In the next section, you will learn how to position and use money as a tool to help you achieve your goals.

Next: Couple Money Skill #2 Make Money Your Ally

$ $ $

Couple Money Skill #2

Make Money Your Ally
(Learn the Importance of Money
& Money Management)

> *"Money is the root of all good."*
>
> —*Ayn Rand, Atlas Shrugged*

I run into people all the time who try to tell me that money is not important. They insist that they are indifferent to money. They say that to care about money is to be cheap and crass, lacking in class. Or they say, "Money isn't everything," as they pay way too much for a product that will take them months, perhaps even years, to pay off.

When I hear what they say, I cannot help but respond: "Wrong! Wrong! Totally wrong!" These are usually the same folks who are barely scraping by, always worrying about money, stressed out about paying their bills, frustrated and in foul moods as they try to squeeze a few more miles out of the bald tires on their car. If they dislike money so much, why do they spend so much time talking about it, thinking about it, and worrying about it? I believe that they are trying to convince themselves of something that makes absolutely no sense. These are often the very same people who are envious of such successful folks as Bill Gates and Donald Trump, and who think that it is a disgrace to be worth a couple of billion dollars. I believe their syndrome is known as "sour grapes" – they do not have money and they have no idea how to obtain it and, most of all, how to manage it. Therefore, they are resentful of those who do.

When these folks berate those who do know how to manage and obtain money, I ask them why they feel that way, and they have no idea. "Well, it's just not right, that's all," one rather down-at-the-heel young lady once told me. She complained about CEOs who received multi-million dollar bonuses and said that people shouldn't be allowed to earn so much money. Now, I confess that I'm not sure some CEOs and professional athletes are worth what they're paid, but I'm not envious or believe it to be morally wrong. The punch line: when I asked this young lady how much people should be allowed to earn, she didn't have a clue. Should it be $10,000 a year? $35,000? These seemed okay to her. She got a bit uncomfortable when I hit the $100,000 mark, and was sure that $1 million a year was way too much. Why? She still didn't know. Who should determine how much everyone earned? No idea. When I suggested that there really was no "wrong" income level, she still didn't agree, but she had no reason.

When it got right down to it, her one and only problem was that they had money and she didn't. And with her attitude, she probably never would. The fact was that she understood nothing about money or about the people she thought of as rich.

This young lady – and way too many people like her – care about money, all right. We all do. Like many of us, however, they are just in a curious love-hate relationship with it. They want money, but they also want to ignore it, to not be thought of as money hungry or materialistically shallow. As the psychologists would say, they have "unresolved issues" with money. So they work all week to earn as much money as they can, but then treat their earnings with disdain, sometimes throwing their paychecks away on worthless junk. They treat money like an enemy, something they certainly need, but generally dislike. If this describes you all or in part, it's time to get over it.

$ $ $

$ $ $

Money Is Good

It is time to make friends with money, to work with it and to get it to work with you and for you. So, let me set the record straight: money is good! Let me repeat that: *money is GOOD!* Whenever I say that to people, the initial response is almost always a universal gasp. We have been told – or at least we think we have been told – that money is evil. Wrong!

Money is good. It determines our standard of living and the physical quality of our life; where we live; what we eat; the type of car we drive; when, where, how and how often we vacation. Money is the fuel that powers our lifestyle. It is money that decides where – and whether – our children go to college. Money is the tool that can get us all the nice material things in life that we want. Beyond that, it is money that allows us to help others, to support our religious house of worship, to take care of our children, to support our favorite charities, to put food on our tables, and to go out for a nice meal on Saturday night.

According to Dr. Dennis E. Hensley, author of *The Power of Positive Productivity: Accelerate Your Success and Create the Life You Want:*

> *Let's get something straight from the start: there is nothing evil or wrong about amassing a fortune by working hard and honestly. The concept of money being dirty or filthy is nonsense.*

A man or woman can be as evil on $1,000 or less a month as he or she can be on $100,000 or more a month and maybe more so. It is his or her attitude toward money and the way that person uses it – for good or evil purposes – not the amount of money itself that he or she earns or accumulates.[8]

So, if you think that money is evil or sordid, now is the time to change your thinking. There is NOTHING evil or crass about money. If you really believe that it is the root of all evil, give up your job, tear up your credit cards, donate your cars and your house to a worthy cause, and move to a desert island where you can live on coconuts you collect yourself and fish you skewer with a handmade spear.

So, let me repeat: money is good. It funds breakthroughs in medical technology that keep you and your children healthy and cure you when you get sick. Money supports businesses that deliver the goods and services that make life so wonderful and reduce hardship. It creates our economy. And, yes, it even generates taxes (I know, ugh!) that pay for the roads you drive on and the schools your children attend. Without money, we would be living miserable lives of squalor in mud huts, with a life expectancy of about 35 years.

Now, do not get me wrong. I am not advocating a crass, brash, materialistic love of money. Far from it. There is nothing less satisfying than money for its own sake. Money will not buy happiness. As Mark Victor Hansen and Robert G. Allen say in *The One Minute Millionaire*: "Clearly, money isn't everything. For us, it's not even in the top four – miles behind family, health, friends, and spiritual values."[9]

The point is that money enables us to accomplish amazing things, starting with the ability to take care of our families. Still feeling a bit uncomfortable? Just for the record, the belief that money is

---

[8] *The Power of Positive Productivity: Accelerate Your Success and Create the Life You Want,* Dennis E. Hensley, PhD, Possibility Press, 2005, p. 41
[9] *The One Minute Millionaire,* Mark Victor Hansen and Robert G. Allen, Harmony Books, 2002, p. ii

the root of all evil comes from an erroneous paraphrasing of the Bible. Specifically, St. Paul did not say that money is the root of all evil. He wrote: "The *love* of money is the root of all evil" (1 Timothy 6:10). Big difference. Very big difference.

So, no, do not value or desire money for its own sake. *That* is shallow and crass. There are those in the world who are obsessed with money and who have goals such as, "I want to be a millionaire by age 40!" or who actually believe that the more money they have, the happier they will be. (I actually tried that once – setting the goal of having a net worth of one million dollars. It was the most non-motivated month of my life. But when I recalibrated my goals in terms of my loved ones – wanting to provide my family with a comfortable home, wanting to make sure my children could attend nice schools, wanting to make sure my wife felt secure from financial worry, all goals that could be accomplished with money – then I was motivated.)

A quick scan through a copy of *People* or some other celebrity gossip magazine will show the fruitlessness of believing that money can buy happiness. At least one article in just about every issue will tell about how the "beautiful people" – blessed with fame and fortune and drop-dead looks – too often live in an endless struggle to find peace and happiness. Our favorite movie star, age 27, swears that this one is for real, as she and hubby number three jet off to a private Greek island after a two million dollar wedding. This is followed by the sad punch line three months later, set in screaming headlines, "Beautiful Star Flees Rocker Hubby."

No, do not fall in love with money. However, do respect and appreciate it for the good it can do, and then start using it to achieve your goals.

$$\$ \$ \$$$

Money Is a Tool

Like a hammer, a computer or a washing machine, money is a tool that can help us build something of value or make our lives easier. It is a tool – no more, no less. However, it is a powerful tool. If you are not careful, it can enslave you, making you toil eight, ten, even fourteen hours a day to acquire it. If you learn how to tame it and master it, however, it will do whatever *you* tell it to do. *You* can decide how it will be used. But like a powerful dog, it must be trained and brought to heel. You can turn it loose and let it fend for itself, in which case it will wander out of your back yard or tear up the house. Or you can train it and put it to work for you, making it your loyal beast. Do that and your money will become a reliable friend that looks after you now and well into the future. All you have to do is tell it what to do. That also means you must know what you want it to do. You can squander it on senseless pleasures that bring no true satisfaction, or you can employ it to achieve your goals and to help you realize your dreams. You can become the master of your money or you can become its servant. The choice is yours.

═══════════════

The Joy of Money

John is a millionaire, though you could never tell just by looking at him. He dresses casually, lives in a nice but unpretentious home, and drives a six-year-old car. He started with nothing and, over the years, has owned several grocery stories, rental properties, and a business supply warehouse, as well as a laundromat. He has always worked hard and is fond of sharing with others his belief that one should "do well by doing good."

He puts his money where his mouth is: he provides low-income housing for less fortunate members of the town, personally funds the Independence Day fireworks celebrations at the community park each year, offers guidance, advice and capital to help ambitious friends and neighbors start their own businesses, and hires people from time to time who need a fresh start in life.

His money has benefited him, his family and the community. On more than one occasion, he has extended credit to customers or tenants who were struggling with financial setbacks. And, yes, on more than one occasion, he has gotten burned. But he works hard to manage his money, and he carefully plans how it will benefit him and others. Without his generous support, dozens of people over the years would have lost their homes or been forced into bankruptcy. Just as important, he has helped improve the quality of life in his community. For John, money is a powerful tool for good.

The Pain of Money

David also worked hard for his money. He was a talented financial planner. He was sharp, ambitious, and likable. However, he became consumed with the need for money, and he never had enough. He once confided to friends that he was designing a new home with a fifteen-hundred-square-foot master bedroom suite, complete with exercise room and sauna. He was driven by his desire for money, and he was one of those guys who believed that sad motto: "He who dies with the most toys, wins!" He earned and spent ... and spent and spent.

Money ruled his life, and he never had enough. Eventually, David began helping himself to his clients' money. He was charged with embezzlement, convicted and, at the age of 33, was sentenced to 18 months in federal prison. He destroyed his own life, ruined his family, and caused harm to countless others, all because he thought money – more and more money – was the key to happiness. Money ran David's life, and he let money ruin it.

Money is a tool. It is how we use money that matters. So, let me stress again that I am NOT saying money can buy happiness or that it has value in and of itself. It cannot and does not. Also, do not confuse living high on the hog with living well and being happy. That is a personal decision. Lack of money can cause a great deal of unhappiness. Worse, poorly managed money can cause hardship. Worst of all, not understanding the strengths and limitations of money can destroy you and others.

The bottom line: forget the notion that money is evil. People who say that either (A) don't have any ... and don't want you to have any, either; or (B) they want to make you feel guilty about having any money ... and then will try to talk you into giving it to them.

Money is not bad. It is just a tool, a very important and powerful tool that can be used by you to accomplish much good. If you have an ambiguous, love/hate relationship with money, now is the time to get over it. Recognize the value of money and start putting it to work to benefit you and those about whom you care.

$ $ $

Wealth Builder #7
Your Attitude Toward Money

What do you think about money? To get a better idea of your attitude regarding this important took, please complete the exercise located in the *Back to Basics Book of Money Workbook.*

$ $ $

$ $ $

Rewarding Yourself

I know, you are working hard here. So, now it's time to start building in a reward. You'll actually do this in the next Wealth Builder, by opening a joint savings account. This will be separate from any other account you have. It will be designated as your "fun-time account" or "personal reward account."

You will then seed it with a small deposit – $10, $20, $50, or whatever small amount with which you are comfortable. You will also earmark that money for an overnight get-away or some other fairly inexpensive item or event in the future that the two of you can enjoy together. This will be a small reward for taking on the challenge of money management.

And that's an important lesson to remember: your money management efforts are not just an exercise in sacrifice. They are intended to make your life better. This is the first reward for all the work you are doing. The point of this is to emphasize that money is a tool…and it can be a fun tool. Use it responsibly for the things you want (even the extravagant luxuries), but never let it enslave you.

$ $ $

Wealth Builder #9
Build Your First Reward for
Responsible Money Management

Build your first reward for responsible money management. It's time to begin building in your own reward system for effective money management. To get started, please complete the exercise located in the *Back to Basics Book of Money Workbook*.

$ $ $

The Bottom Line

Congratulations! You are off to a good start. And it probably was not all that painful. If you feel a bit uncomfortable with these simple tasks and decisions, or if you find it difficult to discuss money with your partner, do not worry. That means you are facing some grim realities that you may have ignored for years, and you are beginning to look at money in a way you may never have considered before.

What's Next: In the next section, you will learn how to begin mastering your money and putting it to work for you by looking at how and why you spend money, and how to begin managing it more effectively.

Next: Couple Money Skill #3 Identify the Leaks in Your Financial Bucket

$ $ $

Couple Money Skill #3

Identify the Leaks in Your Financial Bucket
(Learn Where Your Money Goes Each Month)

> *"Some people wanted champagne and caviar when they should have had beer and hot dogs."*
>
> —*Dwight D. Eisenhower*

In the previous skill section, you learned about the role of money in your life and how it can either be a loyal servant that helps you build assets and enjoy a comfortable standard of living, or a destructive taskmaster that spins your life out of control and at the mercy of every vendor, credit card company and other lender.

The most important lesson you learned is that money is a tool. It is not something you just earn and spend, but something you use to achieve your own specific goals and objectives. So, let's look at a quick, easy way to boost your standard of living almost immediately by identifying and then plugging the "leaks" in your financial bucket.

$ $ $

$ $ $

Identifying the "Leaks" in Your Money Bucket

I have a friend who could not figure out why he was always broke, while "lucky" folks like me always had cash in our pockets, could afford great vacations now and then, and simply lived better. Tired of hearing him gripe, I sat him down one day and made him list his income on one side of a sheet of paper and his expenses on the other. When we added up and compared the two, the belt would not buckle, so to speak. He was spending about $400 more a month than he was earning. As amazing at it may sound, he simply did not realize that there had to be a direct connection between income and outgo, that the good fairy was not going to sprinkle cash into his bank account at some mythical date in the future, that his next raise was not going to solve any of his problems, or that buying lottery tickets each week was more a sign of pathetic desperation than a realistic solution to his money problems.

He did not recognize that if he kept adding more debt each month to live above his means today, those bills would require a sacrifice at some date in the future, whether it was a year from now or ten years down the road. Eventually, he would have to balance his books and live within his means. The more he was in debt, the longer that process would take.

Perhaps the biggest problem most people face – and the easiest to correct – is what I refer to as "leaking" cash. Even minor wastes of money are like a faucet with a slow drip or a bucket with holes in it. No matter how much you keep filling it up, the money just keeps leaking out. Over time, gallons of cash go down the drain. The problem is that many of us spend money without thought or a plan. Those are the leaks. If we have money, we spend it, without giving serious consideration to the value we get for it, a drip here, a drip there.

Let's say you like to dine out at a mid-range restaurant two times a week. The place is convenient, the food is good, the staff knows you by name, and the check never goes beyond $40 for the two of you. Realistically, however, this has become just a habit, albeit a nice one. Still, what would happen if you ate at home just one of those nights? Well, since you would still need to eat, let's say the groceries would come to $10. So, by eating at home just one night a week, you would immediately plug one $30 leak in your money bucket. No big deal, right? Guess again. Over the course of a year, that $30 a week you do not spend saves you $1,500! Plus, you still get to dine out at your favorite restaurant once a week.

Or take that $1.25 candy bar you buy every day. This adds up to $456.25 a year. Now, as a chocolate lover, I consider this a reasonable expense. The point is that if you reined in your chocolate craving and limited your purchases to two candy bars a week, your annual chocolate fix would come to $130. You would fatten your wallet by $326.25 while perhaps thinning down your waistline.

The point is not that you should cut out restaurants or candy bars, but rather that those little expenditures we don't even think about can add up over time. What you spend your money on is your business. However, keep in mind that even minor changes in your spending patterns can make major differences in your money situation. Look around for those leaks in your money bucket, and then look for ways to plug them. Very often, it takes little effort to realize big savings. Don't be surprised if just watching how you spend your money can put an additional $25 or $50 back in your pocket each week. Best of all, this is like found money that can be pocketed with very little effort or sacrifice, and that can be allocated to reducing your debt load, building a college fund for your children, or just spent on something you really do want or need.

Here's another example. Do you keep your thermostat set at 75 degrees in the winter and 70 degrees in the summer? Try dialing your furnace back to 70 degrees in winter (and 66 at night) and set the air conditioner at 75 degrees in the summer. Depending on your typical utility bill, you just might be able to shave 10 percent off the checks you write each month.

Then there is the matter of simply paying more than you need for purchases. Let's say you are in the market for a new mattress and box spring set for your bedroom. If you are like most people, you know little about mattresses. You walk into the showroom, lie down on a few display models, find one that feels pretty good, and then buy it. However, one set that feels pretty darn good may cost $750, while another (perhaps a mis-matched set) that feels just about as good, might be tagged at $625. The decision you make standing there in the showroom will determine who gets that $125 difference, you or the store.

Look at it this way: every dollar you pay to someone else is one less dollar you have to spend on something else! It's your money. You work hard to earn it. Work just as hard to keep it. Start thinking in terms of a nickel here, a dime there, a hundred dollars somewhere else. It adds up. You will find that you are living better on the same income.

$ $ $

The Cause of Money Troubles

If you have money woes, do not blame the bank, the credit card company, your job, the government, or the store that sold you some overpriced do-dad. They are in the business of making money. You should be in the business of keeping your money and spending it frugally. It is up to you to take charge of your finances and decide how you spend your money. Except for taxes and the debts you already have, no one can make you spend your money. If that guy who cuts your lawn raises his rates this summer, you have the right to say, "I like you, Danny, but I can't afford to do business with you anymore," and find someone else to do the job. Or if you stumble across a great deal on a vacation cruise, but even that great deal is more than you really should be spending, you can say no. Find a better way to reward yourself. You can – and usually should – say no at any time to the next invitation to write a check or plunk down your credit card for something you cannot afford or believe the price is too high.

As I mentioned before, most people either give no thought to how they manage money or they think they are pretty good at it. If they are married, they almost always say that their money woes are the result of how the spouse handles – or mishandles – money. I have talked to husbands who spent money like it was going out of style, but looked me straight in the eye and explained that the wife just wasn't any good at money management. And I have talked to wives who complained that the husband wasted money on every new power tool and techno-gizmo that came on the market, while they spent their weekends cruising the malls and filling up closets with clothes that were worn once (at most), kept for a year, and then given to Goodwill.

These blind spots are generally the result of differing attitudes toward what is important. He may feel his new lawn tool is a necessity, but have no interest in his wife's purchase of new curtains for the living room. She may feel that another outfit for the children is vital, but does not understand why her husband shells out several hundred dollars for season sports tickets for his favorite team. I am not here to say that one expenditure is more important than another. Take the position that both of you are spending money on things you want. However, you may both be "leaking" money at every turn. It is time to make compromises.

No finger pointing, please. It gets no one anywhere. That was then; this is now. Remember, as we discussed before, you are in this together. Now it is time to identify the leaks in your financial bucket. Otherwise, you can work all week, even get a second job, and you will never get ahead. So, let's figure out where your money goes every month. Once you know where and how you are spending your money, you can begin to plug those leaks. Otherwise, you risk just muddling along, struggling from paycheck to paycheck, cutting back one month, splurging the next, running full tilt on a money treadmill … and blaming the situation on each other, the bank, the kids, or fate.

Simply identifying where your money goes each month can be frighteningly revealing. It can also be a great motivator to initiate spending pattern changes. You may find that you are leaking thousands of dollars each year and not even knowing it. Just completing the following Wealth Builder may show you how to solve many of your cash flow problems … and begin filling your financial bucket to the brim.

$ $ $

Wealth Builder #11
Your Spending Journal

Now it's time to begin tracking how you currently spend money. To set up and use your spending journal, go to the exercise located in the *Back to Basics Book of Money Workbook.*

$ $ $

What's Next: Over the coming weeks, you will begin see how you have identified leaks in your financial bucket and how you have begun to plug them. That's what we will look at next – how to plug those leaks by getting control of your spending habits, and learning how to use money as a tool, not a toy.

Also, be aware that you can begin this next step while you are still getting a handle on your spending and identifying the leaks in your financial bucket. Besides, you are probably already thinking about ways to cut down expenses.

Next: Couple Money Skill #4 Plug Those Leaks in Your Financial Bucket

$ $ $

Couple Money Skill #4

Plug Those Leaks in Your Financial Bucket
(Learn How to Use Money as a Tool, Not a Toy)

> *"Money! Money! It's like the sun
> we walk under; it can kill
> or it can cure."*
>
> *– Thornton Wilder*

Every dime you do not spend is another ten cents that stays in your pocket … and that can be used to help you achieve your financial goals. It is as simple as that. In this section, we will look at how to cut out wasteful, useless spending and you will learn how to plug those leaks in your financial bucket.

$ $ $

Take a Proactive Approach to Spending

By now, you should have a good idea where your money goes each month. And if you are like many people, a fair amount of it slips through the cracks and gets spent without delivering very much value to you. Dollars and cents leak from the holes in your financial bucket just as your change would if you had a hole in your pocket.

Now imagine, for example, that when you began to track your spending, you found that you are spending $500 a month (that's $6,000 a year!) on products and services that offer you very little if any value or satisfaction. (These will likely be items that come up with ratings of 1-4 on your "spending value criteria" as described in your workbook.) Maybe it's a gym membership you use once a month. Maybe it's buying microwave popcorn that costs about five times more than the stovetop, pop-it-yourself kind. Maybe it's that auto insurance policy with a $50 deductible, but which would save you at least 15 percent on your premiums if you upped the deductible to $250.

Further imagine how your life would improve if you cut expenses and took more control of where and how you spent your money. First of all, you most likely would not even miss the things you are not spending money on. Second, right off the bat, you would have $500 more each month to spend on things you truly wanted. Or you could put all or part of it aside for a college fund, retirement, debt reduction, a new car (Imagine paying cash for your next car!) or a once-in-a-lifetime vacation. And all this can take place with no real reduction in your lifestyle or sacrifice because these were expenditures that were providing very little benefit or satisfaction. They were the result of sloppy spending. So, let's look at how to plug those leaks in your financial bucket by developing a strategy for spending money only on things that provide value.

Keep in mind that controlling your spending can be fun. At the very least, it need not be painful. You don't have to turn off the money stream faucet and live like paupers. On the contrary, the goal is to focus your spending on things you really want, rather than throwing money all over the place and seeing how it works out. In the end, you will live a lot better than you are living today.

$ $ $

Why & How We Spend Money

David and Jackie have a combined household income of less than $45,000 a year. While they do not live extravagantly, they have the means to take at least one long vacation each year, drive a late model car, squirrel away money for retirement and have virtually no debt, except for their mortgage.

53

Cal and Joanie, on the other hand, earn $110,000 a year. However, while they live well, they have almost no money put aside for the future and carry an installment debt load of more than $30,000.

The difference between these two couples is that David and Jackie have mastered the art of proactive money management. They spend with purpose, save with purpose. They are in control of their spending. Cal and Joanie, on the other hand, spend without a plan and without purpose, without rhyme or reason.

Let's take a look at some spending patterns, as well as how to become smart shoppers. Start by recognizing that it can be self-defeating the way some of us spend money: feeling flush and splurging on payday, rummaging through the couch in search of small change by the end of the month. Too often our spending habits reflect how fat or thin our wallets feel. As a result, we often do not get our money's worth for the dollars we spend. We treat money like a toy rather than a tool.

The bottom line: there is a lot more to spending money than many people realize. It drives me nuts to hear friends complain about how broke they are, while they sport designer clothes or drive around town in a car they cannot afford. These are very often the same people who clip coupons for 39 cents off a box of cereal at the grocery, but then spend $495 on impulse for a bistro table and two patio chairs, just because the store put up a big sign near the checkout saying the set was reduced from $575. (They're proud that they saved $80, while they should be ashamed that they wasted $495 on something they hadn't even thought about or wanted before they entered the store.)

The assumption here is that you are probably spending more money than you should, and you are not paying adequate attention to how you spend it. That has a lot to do with the psychology of how we spend money.

$ $ $

The Psychology of Spending

The psychology of spending is more complex than many of us realize. It is like the reasons people eat … or overeat. For example, experts say that thin people eat because they are hungry. However, overweight people eat for every reason *other* than because they are hungry. They are happy. They are sad. They are angry. They are worried about money. They are upset because they are overweight.

It can be the same with money. We spend it because we are sad; because we are happy; because it makes us feel good when we buy something new; because we are bored and decide to go out and just spend money on *something* (it often does not matter what).

I have even seen people spend money because they are worried about money. They take a fatalistic view. I have a friend who owes more than $10,000 on credit card bills and misses payments right and left. His take on his situation is that his finances are so far out of control that it no longer matters. Of course, he is simply putting off his doomsday, but in the meantime, he plans to enjoy himself to the fullest. The last time the bill collectors came knocking on his door, he took his family to Disney World for a week. Before that, after he told me how broke he was, he said he had to go home and set up his new in-home gym. The price: $750! I had very little sympathy for him.

Then there are those who simply decide to "go shopping." The purpose is to spend money and buy stuff. That is a lot different from deciding you need a particular item and then going to the store to buy it. The first activity treats money as a toy and shopping as a sport. The second involves a conscious decision to use money for a needed or desired purchase.

$ $ $

Shopaholism

For some people, spending is a disease known as "shopaholism." It can be as serious and destructive as alcoholism, drug abuse or a gambling addiction. As I mentioned earlier, I had a neighbor whose wife hid credit card bills like alcoholics hide vodka bottles. The more he struggled to pay off the bills she rang up, the more she seemed to spend. She took no responsibility for her spending, while he, at one point, was working three jobs just to keep the bill collectors at bay. They had an ongoing series of tearful discussions, during which – at first, at least – she swore that she would cut back. It never happened. She was addicted to shopping. Meanwhile, they slid ever deeper into debt. She refused counseling, began blaming him, the pressures of life, or her mother (pick a day) for her addiction, and developed a pattern of spending, getting caught, professing dismay and remorse, and then, within a month, going right back to racking up huge bills again.

Their marriage and their lives were dominated by her spending. Obviously, there were other problems at play in her addiction. In the end, it did not matter. Tragically, as he came to the sad conclusion that there was no more he could do, she eventually gave up her two children and husband rather than face her problem. He devoted the next five years to digging out from under their debts. Today he is living comfortably, with no debt. She is renting an apartment, and changing housing every six months or so as her finances and her shopaholism continue to dominate her life.

As we saw above, chronic over-spending can disrupt a family's financial stability. Just as bad, it can lead to guilt and depression and even undermine an otherwise happy marriage. Danger signs include high debt loads, closets full of unused clothes and gadgets, shopping as an escape when feeling down or to celebrate when feeling good. Compulsive spenders tend to shop more from habit, boredom or unhappiness than genuine need. The problem can be serious. Fortunately, in all but the most extreme instances, awareness and a little self-discipline are enough to bring "shopaholic" spending under control.

The above example is extreme. If you or your partner has serious shopaholic tendencies, counseling is in order. But let's assume that you are like the majority of men and women in this country, who see themselves as "consumers." (By the way, that is a terrible phrase, one that assumes your value is not as a person or a parent or spouse, but as a consumer of goods and a spender of money.) You can control your spending. It just takes a strategy and some determination.

$$$

Wealth Builder #12
Shopaholic Self-Quiz

Why do you spend money? Do you have shopaholic tendencies? To find out, complete the exercise located in the *Back to Basics Book of Money Workbook*.

$$$

How to Spend Money

Spending money is easy. The tough part is getting the best value for that money. Consider that most of us work long and hard for the money we earn – 40 hours or more each week, as many as 50 weeks a year. But when it comes to our lifestyle, it is not so much what we earn that counts, but how we spend it. By paying attention to why and how we spend money, it is possible to boost our standard of living by five percent, ten percent, or even more virtually overnight.

There are two good reasons to spend money.

Good Reason #1: Necessity – to provide food, shelter, education, retirement income and other fundamentals for our loved ones and ourselves. This should always get top priority. We spend money to meet our obligations and to provide a respectable standard of living and lifestyle for our families and ourselves.

Good Reason #2: Fun – because the things we purchase give us or others enjoyment. This may include donating money to our favorite charity, jetting off to the islands or just treating ourselves to an evening out. Don't get the misimpression that effective money management means you cannot have fun with your money. On the contrary, it means that you get better value and receive more genuine enjoyment from the money you do spend.

The problem is that there are twice as many
bad reasons to spend money.

Bad Reason #1: Boredom (as in, "I think I'll go shopping"). This reduces spending to a fairly expensive sport or hobby and treats money as a toy.

Bad Reason #2: Indifference ("I have it, so I might as well spend it"). This is also known as the "flush factor," because we tend to spend more freely when we feel flush ... and because we can flush away tidy sums without giving it much thought or getting much value. Or it could be considered mindless impulse spending. If you buy that tempting candy bar – strategically placed at eye level – while standing in line at the grocery store, that's impulse buying, or buying out of indifference.

Bad Reason #3: Comfort ("Shopping makes me feel better about life and myself"). People sometimes spend money because they are angry with a partner or because they're upset and find that shopping makes them feel good. Just as too much comfort food will make you fat, too much comfort spending will make you broke.

Bad Reason #4: Habit ("We always buy a new car every two years"). People sometimes spend large sums of money without even thinking that they do not have to do so. Maybe it's that restaurant they visit every Sunday evening – and spend $50 – just because they always have for the last ten years. If you enjoy it, that's one thing, but if you shell out money simply because you always have, that's a bad and expensive habit.

$ $ $

Wealth Builder #13
Why & How Do You Spend Money?

How and why do you spend your money? Take a few minutes to get a feel for your approach to spending by completing the self-quiz located in the *Back to Basics Book of Money Workbook.*

$ $ $

Deciding Where & How to Spend Your Money

How can you get the best value for the money you spend? There are two "value tests" you can apply to help assure you get your money's worth when you make a purchase, whether it is fast food, a new pair of shoes, a major appliance or a vacation.

Value Test #1: Personal Value

This is a very subjective method of determining value. It helps you determine whether or not you should buy something. It simply involves a matter of making choices based on asking yourself two simple questions:

1. *"Did I get my money's worth?"*

2. *"Would I spend the money again if I had the decision to do over?"*

This goes back to the "spending value criteria" from the last lesson on identifying the leaks in your financial bucket. Even asking yourself these simple questions involves a major shift in shopping patterns for many people because it involves making a conscious decision and an analysis of their purchases. Use it to assess the value of purchases you already made. But also use it to determine whether or not you should make a future purchase.

"Is this worth the money they are asking for it?"

and

"If I went home and thought about it for 24 hours, would I come back and buy this tomorrow?"

This applies whether you are considering spending money on a pound of coffee at the grocery store or that to-die-for spring fashion outfit that snapped your head around at the mall. The real value here is that asking these two questions can help stop impulse spending dead in its tracks. You may decide to make the purchase; you may decide to postpone or skip it altogether. However, you have made a proactive, calculated decision rather than just saw it, bought it, moved on.

Compare this to some people (I know a few) who go shopping at the mall, come home and are surprised by all that they bought. You'd think that someone else had made the purchases the way they ooh and ahh as they open each bag, and even stare at a few with an expression that says, "Now, how did that get in there?"

Value Test #2: The PQS Value

This second value test, The PQS Value (PQS stands for Price, Quality, Service) method, is a much more objective way to determine value. It helps you get the best value for an item or service you have already decided to purchase. It is based on the way goods and services are sold. For instance, why will you pay $450 for a television at one retailer, but $375 at another? And are there times when you should pay the higher price? Or have you ever faced the dilemma of shelling out $1,500 per person for a winter vacation on one cruise line versus $1,100 on another? What accounts for the difference?

The answer can be determined by a simple formula based on three factors: *quality, price* and *service.* The general rule is that you can definitely obtain one of these – high quality, low price or excellent service. You can even receive two if you are a smart shopper, which is our goal. However, you will almost never receive all three. (However, the internet is bringing about major ways people buy and businesses sell products and services, to the point that, in an increasing number of situations, it is possible to get quality, price AND service!)

Still, in most situations, you may have to sacrifice service if you want good quality at a low price; or expect to pay a higher price to obtain a high quality product and top quality service. While there will always be exceptions, this general rule is still a good way to measure the value you are getting for the money you spend on goods and services. Your goal should be to make your purchase based on the two factors that are *most* important to you.

Using the Price-Quality-Service (PQS) value test, you can expect to receive only *two* of these factors on a regular basis.

GOOD QUALITY	GOOD PRICE	GOOD SERVICE
YES	YES	NO
YES	NO	YES
NO	YES	YES

For example:

- If you buy an appliance from a wholesaler's warehouse, you may get good price and good quality, but do not waste your breath trying to get service if the thing breaks down.

- If you buy clothes at a discount chain, you may get a good price and good service (through a no-hassle return and exchange policy), but the goods may be of low quality compared to, say, a high-prestige boutique (which may specialize in high quality and personal service, but at a higher price).

- If you buy a top quality car with a super service package from a Main Street dealer, you will generally pay more than if you purchase the same vehicle at $100 over invoice from Discount Dan's, who may not even have a service department.

- If you go out to dinner, you may be able to save money by going to a fast-food restaurant, but you will not get personalized table service from a waiter like you would at an upscale establishment, which may provide impeccable service, table cloths and silverware, but at a significantly higher price.

Apply the formula by deciding which factors are important to you. This is all based on circumstances and what you value. Keep in mind that the criteria will vary depending on the item and your personal situation. A carryout pizza for dinner at mid-week may be reasonably priced, which is what you want. However, when you go out for a romantic dinner on Saturday night, perhaps you want to be pampered, and are willing to pay for that service.

Can you get all three? Can you get quality, price AND service? Yes! But you must either really hunt like a bloodhound or be patient and wait. Personally, I like to keep a list of large items I would like to own, but which I am in no rush to purchase. (Also, I am always looking for that great deal on everyday items, such as that 12-pack of paper towels for two-thirds off.) Then when that item shows up – maybe it's on clearance, maybe it's the end-of-month special – I make my purchase.

The point: by being tuned in to how to shop for value, and being aware of your objectives and needs, you can control the quality and price of the goods and services you purchase ... and get the best possible value for the money you spend.

$ $ $

Establish the Right Attitude

Take up the challenge of money management. Attitude is crucial. Determine to *always* get your money's worth for the dollars you spend. In this week's meeting with your partner, discuss ways to be smart shoppers and spenders. Make sure you are in agreement on the importance of cutting back and/or focusing on how you manage and spend money. This is crucial, because success may require some sacrifice, and that means cooperation from other members of your family.

At the same time take a proactive approach to spending. Begin spending based on conscious decision and need, not cash flow. Do not look for reasons to shell out money just because you have it. Instead, identify what you honestly want and need to buy, or what really brings satisfaction for the money you spend. No more going out just because you always have in the past and no more "going shopping" trips to the mall. Never again make an impulse buy.

Look for alternatives to spending, a substitute to shopping. Some people believe they cannot have fun without spending money. They are wrong. Go to the beach, a library, or a museum; take a walk in a park, rent a movie rather than go out to the movie theater or, better yet, borrow a DVD from the library for free rather than rent one from the video store, or just watch television at home; read a book together or invite friends over to play cards or a board game at home. All this can be just as relaxing as spending $80 on an evening out. This need not require a dramatic lifestyle shift. Do not give up *all* the things that cost money. Just start cutting back. And keep track of the money you are saving.

$ $ $

Wealth Builder #14
Can You Have Fun Without Spending Money?

The answer is yes! Go to the exercise in the *Back to Basics Book of Money Workbook,* and list some things you can enjoy without spending a boatload of money.

$ $ $

$ $ $

The Bottom Line

Awareness is perhaps the greatest single factor when it comes to plugging those leaks in your financial bucket. Think before you spend. Precede each purchase with a proactive decision, not just an impulse. Follow these steps and you may be surprised how easy it is for you to end up with an additional $50, $75, maybe even $100 more in your pocket at the end of the week.

What's Next: Learning how to spend your money only on the products and services that give you genuine value is crucial. Just as important is learning how to control debt and use credit as a tool to help you achieve your goals. In the next lesson, we will look at how to use credit, how to stop adding new debt and start paying off accumulated debt, and when and how to borrow money.

Next: Couple Money Skill #5 Treat Debt as a Curable Disease

$ $ $

Couple Money Skill #5

Treat Debt as a Curable Disease
(Learn How to Use Credit, Not Abuse It)

> *"I owe! I owe!*
> *So off to work I go!"*
>
> —*Bumper Sticker*

Paper or Plastic?

Paper or plastic? At the grocery story, that may be an arbitrary decision.   However, when it comes to paying for those purchases, the answer should always be paper … as in cash. And not just at the grocery store, but everywhere, including department stores and, yes the car dealership. However, the trends are going in the exact opposite direction. Thirty years ago, if people had credit cards at all (and most of us actually got along quite nicely without them), they had one, maybe two. And they could be used at a limited number of places (mostly restaurants and gas stations) to pay for a limited number of items (mostly food and gas).

These days, however, more and more people use credit cards for just about every purchase – from the grocery store to the doctor's office. So, let's make this simple. Whipping out plastic at every turn is a bad habit, one that can cause you to lose control over your money management. That's because charging purchases makes it easy to spend, spend, and spend some more … and that creates debt. It is not an exaggeration to say that in our society, debt has become a disease, more like an addiction. Fortunately, as with many diseases and all addictions, this one is curable. Still, the cure can be painful. Estimates vary, but many households carry as much as $10,000 in consumer debt. What's worse, couples are making minimum payments, and the more they owe, the more many lenders are willing to let them borrow.

They run the risk of getting into a vicious cycle, because the more they owe, the tougher it is to dig out of the financial pit into which they keep sinking deeper and deeper each month.

This is a terrible and totally unnecessary drain and a strain on their standard of living. The real irony is that, for many people, it is not necessarily that they cannot afford to pay off what they owe. It is just that they get used to owing the money and think that paying a small fortune in interest each year is normal. ("Well, yes, all my friends are in debt, too.") They just don't give debt elimination any serious thought, or they have never imagined what it would be like to walk around with zero debt. So, they keep paying, shelling out money to some credit card lender, with money they could probably use for themselves or their children.

We've been over this before, but it's worth repeating. Imagine owing $10,000 on your credit cards and paying 1.5 percent a month in interest, or 18 percent annually. That means you pay $150 each and every month in interest alone before you even begin to reduce the principal. Plus, that $150 a month adds up to at least $1,800 a year in interest.

I know one couple who no longer uses credit cards. They pay cash and write checks for everything, including hotels and airline tickets. (Yes, you can send a check to an airline.) Ten years ago, they were credit junkies, using plastic for just about everything. They justified their plastic addiction by claiming they got airline miles and 5 percent discounts. But that didn't begin to counterbalance the 18 percent interest rates they were paying. They gradually became addicted to credit cards and installment loans, deferring payment on everything they bought. They ended up declaring bankruptcy and coming close to filing for divorce.

The bankruptcy forced them to use cash. It drove them crazy at first, like drug addicts cut off from their supply. However, they claim (and I've seen it) that this was the best wake-up call they ever could have received. They were forced to clean up their financial act. Today, they are financially healthy, have their home paid off, travel extensively (travelers checks work just fine), carry zero balances on their credit cards, borrow installment debt only when it truly benefits them, and other than that, have no debt except for their mortgage. When they must use credit, the bill is paid off each month. They've never been more financially healthy or more personally happy.

Then there are those couples that play a dopey game that they know they will lose before they even start. I've seen it dozens of times. They buy an item, let's say a super-duper, state-of-the-art, flat-screen television set that covers the entire wall and sets them back $2,400. They can't afford it, but the "good" news is that they can purchase it on credit, with no interest or payments and no money due for the next 24 months. The store salesperson is willing (downright eager is a better term, since he or she gets a nice fee for getting you to open your account) to help them fill out the forms. And presto. They're approved within two minutes. Smiles all around. And no payments or interest for two years! Wow!

Then the self-delusion game starts. Two years is a lifetime away, so that those 24 months will never pass. Or somehow, some way, the money will come along – a raise, a windfall (there is always the lottery), or the money fairy will sprinkle them with cash. So, they enjoy their new super system and forget about the money. Now, they *could* pay off that purchase over the next two years by writing a check for $100 a month. If they did that, they would have bought the television, borrowed the money (at zero interest, no less) and spread their payments over two years. That would have been a smart purchase. However, all too often, and all of a sudden, two years have passed (where did the time go?) and they suddenly owe $2,400 right now. Of course, they do not have the money (the darn money fairy never showed up ... or if she did, they spent the money somewhere else), so they suddenly discover (what they knew all along) that because they did not pay off the debt, they have accumulated – retroactively over the last two years – a whopping 25 percent interest charge on the money. So, now they owe $3,750! And that rate of 25 percent continues until they pay off the whole amount, which now will probably take them another five years and several thousand dollars more in interest.

Does this sound familiar? If so, you are not alone. (And, no, that does NOT mean it is okay.) Many people do this to themselves each year. And then they act surprised, then get angry at the finance company, and then just hunker down and keep paying … and paying … and paying.

$ $ $

If You Can't Afford to Pay Cash, You Can't Afford to Buy It!

A long time ago, when writing my very first article about money, a man whose name I've long since forgotten (but who I will never forget nonetheless), gave me the most important bit of common sense advice about money that I've ever heard, before or since: if you can't afford to pay cash, you can't afford to buy it!

If you remember this and nothing else from this book, you will be on the road to solid financial health: if you can't afford to pay cash, you can't afford to buy it.

Can you do that? Can you do away with debt and make it stay away? You bet you can! And it is time to stop carrying unnecessary debt from month to month and paying a fortune in interest. Instead, start paying off your debts. For many people, onerous debt is like a 500 lb. gorilla sitting on their backs. It started out as a small monkey, but just kept getting bigger and bigger … and hungrier and hungrier. I know people who keep getting deeper into debt and end up devoting 10, 20, 30 percent of their income to interest and credit card payments. What a waste of money!

The problem with debt is that it MUST be paid back. If you pay it today, the interest you are shelling out to maintain that debt

69

goes away. If you pay it later, or just carry a ton of debt year after year, as some people are inclined to do, you will pay an additional 5 percent, 10 percent, 15 percent or higher for that privilege. So, why not pay it off now and give yourself a raise of that 5 percent, 10 percent, 15 percent or higher?

What happens when you become debt-free? All that money can now go to living better, boosting your standard of living. You have back in your own pocket all that interest you've been paying to everybody else, money that can now go for your own use and enjoyment.

But I don't want to reduce my lifestyle, you say. I like to buy a new car every two years, shop for new clothes every weekend, buy new electronic gizmos that come on the market. If so, go ahead, but if you are living above your means, remember that you are living in a house of cards. If you do not take the time now to replace and rebuild it by practicing proven money management skills, it will eventually – in one year, five years, maybe even a decade from now – tumble down around you, leaving you financially devastated.

A better idea: take charge of your financial life right now. Start reducing debt and building true wealth immediately. In the long run – in one year, maybe five years, maybe even a decade from now – you will be financially solid and personally better off in pretty much every way.

So, let's get to work understanding the concept of debt and credit cards.

$ $ $

The Psychology of Plastic

As I mentioned earlier, you can live without credit cards. The concept is simple: if you can't afford to pay cash, you can't afford to buy it! Any questions? This is one of the most important rules of financial health. Forget all the rationalizations about using credit. Sure, you get bonus points and cash back. Sure, you get frequent flyer miles or other discounts. Sure, this can work IF you pay off your balance each and every month. If you are already in complete control of your financial management and have the self-discipline to use credit as a tool to your benefit, you might consider taking advantage of some of these teaser advertising gimmicks. However, if you do not have control of your finances, if you carry ANY balance on your credit card from month to month, any gains you get from these glitzy lures are not worth it. Think otherwise, and you are like the alcoholic who says, "Well, one drink won't hurt." It will. So, if you are paying off your credit cards each month, then and only then, consider using plastic. Still, the smart money says: why would you want to?

And by the way, debit cards are not much better. Like credit cards, debit cards make it easier to make unplanned purchases, and that makes them a bad choice. To help stop spending money willy-nilly, stop using debit cards. Plus, in many cases, debit cards are also tied to overdraft protection. This is a valuable tool when used properly. However, it can be one more financial pitfall when used improperly. I know some people who have overdraft protection on their checking or savings account. They are tickled pink because they think that means they can spend more than they have in their accounts. What that really means is that the bank or credit union will gladly lend them money, even if they have no money in their accounts. Oh, and about those overdraft charges? The interest rate is no gift. It's debt.

The real problem with credit cards is that they take away the reality of spending. (If you have ever played blackjack in a casino, the concept is the same. The house converts your cash into chips. And almost invariably, at some point, someone will make a questionable bet and announce, "Well, it's only money," only to have the other folks at the table correct him, "No, it's not money; it's only chips.") Credit cards break the mental connection between affordability and spending. Unfortunately, the real connection between those two cannot be broken … just ignored for a limited period of time.

That's one reason stores are so eager to issue you new cards every time you turn around. As you walk in the front door, there will be a table with one or two incredibly charming, smiling employees to greet you. They will also offer you an immediate 10 percent discount on every purchase you make today with the new store credit card they will help you apply for. (I know one woman who has six credit cards from one major department store, and I suspect there are many people out there who have more than that.) They do this for two reasons. First, it will encourage you to shop at their store. Second, it will encourage you to spend more money. When you find something you like, there's no excuse that says you cannot afford it. After all, you have their credit card. Sure, you have to pay it back, but that's a problem for next month.

The bottom line: a credit card creates the illusion that you can do what you want when you want. It's a false power trip. Ultimately, it reduces your power and control over your finances and your life. Oh, and another problem: in case I haven't mentioned it already (and I think I may have) using credit cards will generally cost you hundreds – maybe even thousands – of dollars each year in unnecessary interest payments. Let's say you spend $1,200 a year in interest. Couldn't you find better use for an extra $100 a month? Stuff it in your wallet or purse and go to the mall to buy something you really want. That's real power! Being able to pay cash for the things you want.

$ $ $

How to Stop Adding New Debt

The first step when it comes to getting out of debt is to stop adding new debt. Stop borrowing money. The problem for many people is that they decide to pay off a big chunk of installment debt one month, but then go right back out and add new debt the next. Or they pay off card A while running up bills on card B. This keeps them on the financial treadmill ... running faster and faster, but getting nowhere. So, it's time to get out of the mindset that says you should buy everything and anything on credit. Instead, change your mindset to one that says you should buy NOTHING on credit.

$ $ $

Wealth Builder #16
Stop Adding New Debt

It's time to stop adding new debt. Go to the *Back to Basics Book of Money Workbook* and complete the next exercise to learn how to give up the debt habit.

$ $ $

What's Next: There are two sides to the coin when it comes to debt. The first, as you have just learned, is to stop adding new debt and going on a cash basis for your household. This will take some getting used to, but you will soon become comfortable with this method of managing your expenditures. The next step is to begin whittling away at your exiting debt, with the goal of bringing it down to zero and, eventually, putting those interest and principal payments you are currently making back into your pocket for your own benefit.

Next: Couple Money Skill #6 Pay Off Your Existing Debts

$ $ $

Couple Money Skill #6

Pay Off Your Existing Debts
(Learn How to Put Those Payments
in Your Pocket Instead)

> *"Rich people buy luxuries last,*
> *while the poor and middle class*
> *tend to buy luxuries first."*
>
> *—Robert T. Kiyosaki,*
> *Rich Dad Poor Dad*

Even when you stop adding new debt, your existing debts still exists. It can eat you alive. That's because, as you certainly know, just having debt adds new debt, thanks to the perils of racking up compound interest charges. Later in this book, we will look at ways to grow your money by *earning* interest. For now, let's see what we can do to reduce and eventually eliminate the interest charges you are currently paying by developing a strategy for paying off your debt.

$ $ $

Do the Math: Pay Off Your Old Debts

As I said earlier, for many people, onerous debt is like a 500-pound gorilla on their backs. It started out as a small monkey, but kept getting bigger … and bigger. I know people who keep getting deeper into debt. In the end, they wind up devoting 10, 20, 30 percent of their income to interest and credit card payments. Each month, they have a decreasing amount of money available for themselves. As their debt increases, it is like a noose tightening around their necks.

You next challenge is to start paying off the debts you currently have. We will skip the mortgage and any car loans for the moment. Instead, let's focus on your installment debt.

This is where some sacrifice may be required. On one hand, you will not be adding new debt. That's the easy part. You simply switch from using credit cards to paying cash for each purchase.

Now for the tough part. You need to begin allocating a portion of your income to whittling down – actually eliminating – your current debt load. No, we will not do this all at once. It will take time, perhaps several years. Still, this very likely will cut into your current standard of living and lifestyle for a while. Additionally, it will not seem like you are making any headway at first. Borrowing money is easy and fun. Paying it back can be a drag. It may not seem like much when you reduce the amount of interest you pay each month on your credit card from $125 to $122. However, that really is a big deal. If you are paying 1.5 percent a month in interest, reducing your interest by $3 means you have dropped your debt load from $8,333 by $8,133, or by more than $200. Yes, it will take time to drop it to zero, but you are on the right track, and you will get there. It will just take some time, discipline and determination.

So, here's a little pep talk. It's not just meant to make you feel good, but to help you understand that every day in which you do NOT add more debt and every month that you REDUCE the debt you currently have by even a fraction, this brings you that much closer to full financial health and control of your money. Now here's the real punch line: this isn't something you can avoid. You can put it off, but if you do, your situation will only get worse. Whether you address it now or ten years from now, it will be waiting for you. And ten years from now may be too late for a full recovery.

Do the math. Let's say you have been adding $250 of new debt each month – an extra dinner out here, shopping spree there, a what-the-heck-spur-of-the-moment vacation as an anniversary surprise. That's less than $10 a day in new debt. Big deal. And okay, you're spending the money on stuff that sounds pretty reasonable. But – and this is a math equation you will start doing in your head in your sleep pretty soon – that $250 a month adds up to $3,000 of new debt in one year. If you have been doing this for two years, your total debt load is $6,000, plus the interest, which can bring it well over $7,500. Now let's say you begin paying off $200 a month (while not adding any new debt). That means you can be debt-free in somewhere between three and four years.

That may seem like a long time, but let's see what happens if you continue that same negative pattern year after year of adding just $10 a day in new debt until you have doubled that debt load to around $15,000! For one thing, if your interest rate is 18 percent, you will be paying $2,700 a year in interest alone. Even if you pay $200 a month ($2,400 a year), you will continue to fall behind, continuing to slide ever deeper into debt. Even if you pay $300 a month, it will take you about 15 years to pay off that debt. And that assumes that you totally change your spending habits. Plus, by the end, you will have paid to the lender thousands and thousands of dollars in interest.

Do it now or do it later. The choice is yours. However, if you are serious about improving your financial health, sleeping better at night and enjoying a stress-free (or at least stress-reduced) relationship in your home, the time to start is now. It's never going to get better than right now. It's not going to get better at the first of the year when you get your next raise. It's not going to get better once the kids are out of the house and on their own. It's not even going to get better if a rich uncle dies and leaves you a small fortune. Why? Because if your spending patterns are so established that you are now relentlessly and stubbornly living above your means, there is no reason to believe that those destructive patterns will suddenly go away by themselves, no matter how much money you have.

In fact, I've seen people living in hope of that year-end bonus or inheritance. By the time it arrived, they had spent the money two or three times over, and then they figured, "Why bother to pay off the debts with the money. Let's go spend it on something else. We deserve it!"

In short, you have one reasonable choice: change your money management patterns today and begin knocking down that debt load. That also means using all or part of that raise you will get at the first of the year, the money you will save once the kids are out of the house, and the inheritance you might receive from your rich uncle – use it to pay off debts and build financial health.

$$\$ \$ \$$$

When You Become Debt-Free...

Now let's look at the positive side of this issue. What happens when you eliminate your debt, not just bring it to a reasonable, tolerable level, but reduce it to zero? All that money you have been paying in interest and principal reduction can then go to living better, boosting your standard of living, and giving you true prosperity, not the false kind that comes from living on borrowed time and money. You will then have all that interest you had been paying for your own use.

Or how about if you put that money aside, investing it (more on that later) so that it earns interest rather than costs you money? Imagine putting aside $3,000 each year and earning 10 percent return. That money will double to $6,000 in just over seven years. And you don't have to lift a finger to make it happen, except select safe and reliable investments. Here's a rule we will discuss later: it is always better to earn interest than to pay it.

Angie & Aaron Proved You Can Live on Cash

Angie and Aaron were tired of running on the earn-and-spend-and-run-up-debt treadmill. They decided to eliminate all their debt, with the exception of their mortgage. They had approximately $5,000 in installment debt from credit cards and several appliances. They put away all their credit cards, and set a goal of eliminating that $5,000 debt in three years, which they determined was a reasonable goal.

They allocated a modest $300 to debt reduction each month, or $3,600 a year. They could have afforded more; however, they saw no need to reduce their standard of living to the poverty level. They still wanted to continue enjoying their life AND eliminate their debt at the same time. Yes, they had to cut back on their spending in some areas and make some tough decisions. Still, by the end of the first year, they had reduced their debt to $2,000. Another eight months later, and they had paid off the last of their debt. Not bad for 20 months of focused money management.

Now they had that "extra" $300 a month to do with as they chose. They decided to reward themselves by putting half ($150) into a vacation fund, which gave them $3,600, plus interest, for a fabulous cruise in just two years, enabling them to pay cash for the entire adventure. The rest, that other $150 a month, they used for ongoing, daily lifestyle enhancement ... sometimes known as fun!

Bonus: as they learned to manage their money better and pay off their debts, they found that it was no sacrifice at all. They struggled at first as they worked to get used to living on a slightly reduced spending amount. However, they adjusted, and then were downright tickled when they had that additional $300 of "found" money each month.

What about Declaring Bankruptcy?

The single-word advice on bankruptcy is … DON'T! There may be times when declaring bankruptcy is a good decision. However, in the vast majority of circumstances, bankruptcy is a sign that people have been living way beyond their means, got caught, and have learned nothing. Just as bad, it's not as easy as many people think. You don't get to walk away with much, if anything of your current assets. Plus, this black mark stays on your credit report for the next seven years. Try to borrow money with that on your record. If you can borrow, the interest rate will be sky high.

There are two types of bankruptcy. Under Chapter 7, your debts are discharged completely and need not be repaid. However, some debts may not be included. Under Section 13, your debts are renegotiated. You may be able to eliminate some. However, you generally have three to five years to settle up on the remaining amount. In both cases, the courts determine how your debts are to be discharged. It is no a free-and-clear release from liability.

Here is the biggest reason you should not rush to declare bankruptcy: if you declare bankruptcy today and do not change your spending patterns, you will accomplish nothing in the long run. You will simply wipe out your credit worthiness and continue to damage your financial stability. Too often, people who spend money irresponsibly and then seek relief by declaring bankruptcy end up declaring it again seven years later. They go through life wasting money and never accumulating real wealth.

Filing bankruptcy is not always inappropriate. If you have a large amount of unsecured debt (such as credit card debt), with no hope of ever paying it all off, bankruptcy may be the answer. However, keep in mind that secured debt (debt connected to particular assets) may not be wiped out. You could either be required to continue paying this debt, or risk losing the assets themselves. Second, if you become unemployed or accumulate a large amount of medical bills that you will not be able to address, bankruptcy will give you a fresh start. In most situations, bankruptcy is truly a last resort.

$ $ $

Check Your Credit Report

True Story #1: John checked his credit report before applying for a loan. He found a $40,000 college loan with a spotty payment history. The problem: it wasn't his. It belonged to a total stranger who had a Social Security number *almost* identical to that of his daughter, for whom he had co-signed a loan two months earlier. He also found nearly a dozen other errors, from wrong past addresses to telephone numbers to optional spellings of his name.

True story #2: Tom ordered his credit report. It was sent by mail – with all his personal information in one envelope – to the wrong person in a neighboring city. Fortunately, that person happened to be his son, who brought the documents to him the next day.

Amazing? No, all too common. Keep in mind that, without our permission or knowledge, credit bureaus collect sensitive financial and legal information about us every day. This data is shared with lenders, would-be employers, and others to help them make decisions regarding our credit worthiness and integrity.

Identity theft is one problem. Security is much more lax than you may think. (Imagine if Tom's credit report had been sent to a stranger with less-than-sterling scruples.) Plus, to get your report – or that of anyone else – all you need is a Social Security number, e-mail address, credit card (to purchase the report, though you are eligible for one free report a year, starting this year) and some very basic information about your own borrowing history.

Then there is the problem of simple, human error. Someone, somewhere, keys in a wrong number. You could spend months clearing up a mistake someone else made. That's why it is important to check your credit report each year.

By the way, there is no need to check your credit score. By law, credit bureaus must provide you with your credit report, upon request, once a year at no charge. However, they can charge for (A) letting you monitor your report on an ongoing basis; and (B) providing your credit score. You need neither of these services. If you take out a loan, and they check your credit report, ask the lender for a copy of your report and your scores.

Also check your minor children's reports. Sometimes, would-be crooks pick a Social Security number from a child. Unless you check, it can be used for years before the theft is discovered. Imagine your 18-year-old son applying for his first credit card, only to learn that he is a credit disaster.

$$$

Wealth Builder #17
Check Your Credit Report

It's time to learn about your credit worthiness. To do this, complete the next exercise located in the *Back to Basics Book of Money Workbook*.

$$$

How to Protect Your Credit Rating

Even though you are weaning yourself off the plastic habit, you still need to protect your credit rating. That is because when you do need to borrow money, you want to be sure you get the loan … and to get it at the best possible rate. That is why it is important to maintain a sound credit rating.

Here are several simple steps to help you maintain a good credit rating:

1. Pay your bills on time. This is the single most important factor in determining your rating. If you have a problem meeting payments, contact the people you owe. Otherwise, make sure all payments reach the lender by the due date.

2. Don't ignore mistakes. If you suspect an error, contact the lender immediately, before it is reported to the credit bureau. You may want to start with a phone call, but be sure to ask for verification in writing. Also, when you talk to someone, get his/her full name and extension. If that is not possible (some companies like to know all about you, but protect the privacy of their employees), ask for a verification number.

3. Don't ignore problems. If your debt load is so high that you are having trouble meeting payments, contact the lender and negotiate a reduced monthly payment. Most lenders will work with you ... but you have to contact them to work out arrangements. The worst thing you can do is skip payments. The price you pay goes far beyond the additional interest. You can damage your credit rating for years to come. Plus, some credit companies will jack up your rate if you miss a payment.

4. Follow standard payment procedures to avoid communication problems. Use envelopes provided, when possible. Otherwise, be sure to double check mailing the

address. Be sure to enclose the payment stub. Or pay your bills online. This is the easiest way to assure payment. However, remember that if something goes wrong (such as you forget to click the final "send payment" button), you have no canceled check or other record that you paid the bill.

5. When you do borrow money (and at this point, you should not be adding new debt) stay within pre-approved credit limits. Contact the lender if you need to extend your available credit. Pushing indiscriminately above your limit makes lenders nervous.

6. Check your credit report every year. You have the right to have errors corrected. Also, you can add a statement of up to 100 words to your file explaining disputes or extenuating circumstances involving a credit problem.

7. Don't share information freely. Remember, when you give out your credit card number, a stranger has access to your funds. Even reputable firms sometimes have untrustworthy employees. Check statements carefully each month for unaccountable charges.
8. Watch out for fraud and credit card theft. It's become big business in this country. Always guard your credit information.

$ $ $

When You Have to Borrow Money

If you haven't figured it out by now, here it is again: the basic rule is that debt is bad! Do not take on debt arbitrarily or out of habit. In general, try to avoid debt at all costs. However, that being said, there are times when borrowing money is necessary, sometimes the smart choice ... provided you do it right and for the right reasons.

Paying cash is the best option for most expenses in our daily lives. Many people even purchase big-ticket items with cash ... and that includes paying for vacation cruises and new cars. They do it by building up a cash cushion that can be used to pay for vacations or defray the cost of replacing appliances and meeting financial emergencies.

Nonetheless, there are times when borrowing is the best or at least necessary choice, especially if (1) you are looking at paying the cost of college for your children and have not stockpiled the money in advance; (2) you need a new car and have not piggy-banked the money in advance; or (3) you have an emergency, such as the roof of your house falls in or the transmission in your car falls out.

Smart money managers follow six basic rules when they borrow money:

Rule #1: They never borrow for luxuries. Whether it's a weekend getaway or a piece of jewelry for a loved one, they always pay cash. Instead of borrowing, set up special savings accounts to pay for these luxuries.

Rule #2: They never use credit cards or debit cards for routine purchases. Instead, smart money managers set up spending plans that reflect their income and expenses.

Rule #3: They never borrow money without knowing how they will repay the loan. For example, if they borrow $10,000 for their child's college expenses, they work out a strategy for repayment, such as (A) maintaining interest payments, if any, during the college years; and then (B) paying off the entire remaining amount within, say, four years. They realize that they can't borrow their way out of debt. If they find themselves in over their heads, they know that reducing spending and paying off debts, not borrowing more, is the only solution.

Rule #4: They use credit cards to protect themselves. When there may be a question about the quality of goods or services, a credit card is often the best way to protect the buyer. However, they have the cash on hand to pay off the debt each month, or as soon as is reasonably possible. Some couples use one credit card for making online purchases. Still others – and this is the preferred way – set up PayPal accounts that allow them to shift money from their accounts into their PayPal account.

Rule #5: They carry one credit card with them for emergencies. If they are on vacation 500 miles from home and the car leaves its transmission in the middle of the road, they had better have their credit card around. But only use it for an emergency.

Rule #6: They may borrow money when they can get a good deal on it and can conserve their own cash reserves. For example, it may be worthwhile to take advantage of "90 days same as cash" opportunities when buying a new computer, sound system, or appliance, provided the debt is retired before the interest-free period expires. However, if they have ever done this and ended up paying interest for any reason, they should not try it again. They should play it safe and avoid engaging in a game of "financial chicken" with lenders. Also, keep in mind that sellers sometimes mark up the item's price before offering those terms, so the buyer really saves nothing. It is best to negotiate the lower price AND insist on the free loan. Another time when borrowing money may be a good idea is when the opportunity arises to take out interest-deferred college loans, even if the money is on hand.

The bottom line: debt is a tool. When recognized as such, and used wisely, it can help you achieve your financial objectives. Still, in the vast majority of situations, pay cash for everything.

$ $ $

How to Borrow Money

When you must borrow money, or it fits into your overall financial strategy, keep in mind the following:

1. **Rates vary from lender to lender.** It pays to shop around. Unless someone is giving you "free" money for a period of time, contact at least three institutions. Fortunately, these days, you can do a lot of the shopping for loans online. But also be sure to visit your local financial institution. Many are eager to keep their customers happy, and that means waiving fees.

2. **Rates vary from borrower to borrower.** The lower your credit report, the higher the interest rate you will pay. However, the rate also reflects what the lender senses the "market will bear." If you do not appear to be concerned about the rate you pay, you may pay a higher rate. Ask for the lowest rate.

3. **Negotiate fees.** When I refinanced my mortgage a few years ago, the loan officer promised me the world and mentioned that my closing costs would run about $1,000. I smiled, thanked him, and mentioned that I would have to shop around. All but $150 of those fees magically disappeared.

4. **Negotiate rates.** Regardless of your credit rating, insist on the rate the lender gives its very best customers. The worst they can say is "no." But very often, especially if you make it clear – and do make it clear – that you are shopping around…well, money talks and money walks.

5. **It may pay to borrow against the equity in your home,** although I suggest this with great caution. The advantage is that any interest you pay is tax deductible. The drawback is that you are using your home as collateral for the loan. Some people use their homes as if

they were savings accounts. Over decades, rather than being able to celebrate with a mortgage burning party, they end up carrying a mortgage and home equity loans on their backs, with almost no principal reduction. I know one couple who bought their home in 1978 for $128,000 with 10 percent down and a 30-year mortgage for the remaining $115,200. Over the next 30 years, the home increased in value to more than $550,000. So, in 2008, the year their mortgage was due to be retired, they should have had no debt and an asset worth $550,000. Wrong. Over the years, they had refinanced repeatedly, pulling out market value appreciation time and again. As a result, at the end of that 30-year period, they had a mortgage of $495,000, and equity of approximately $55,000. Worst of all, when the housing market tumbled in 2008, they ended up owing more than the house was worth.

The moral to the story: if you do use a home equity loan or line of credit, or refinance when rates decline, do so with great caution, and be very wary of borrowing the appreciation from your home.

6. **Watch out for *teaser* rates.** These are promotional come-on rates that are adjusted upward within a few months. These are almost always a good deal for the lender and almost always a terrible deal for the borrower. If you must borrow money, think long term, not just a few months ahead.

7. **Go for the shortest repayment period** you can reasonably afford. Interest on borrowed money, even if the rate is attractive, can add up. The shorter period of time that you owe the money (in other words, the sooner you pay it back), the less you will pay in the long run.

$$$

Wealth Builder #18
Create Your Debt Elimination Strategy

Let's figure out the exact date when you plan to be totally debt-free. To do this, complete the next exercise located in the *Back to Basics Book of Money Workbook*.

$ $ $

What's Next: You have come a long way. You have been addressing a number of financial challenges and setting objectives. However, it all probably seems a bit random. In the next section, you will learn how to bring all your previous money management decisions together – learning how to pay bills, how to set up and use a spending plan, and even how to manage a potential windfall, whether it comes from an inheritance, tax refund or the right number combo in the multi-big-bucks lottery.

Next: Couple Money Skill #7 Manage Your Money

$ $ $

Couple Money Skill #7

Manage Your Money Like It Counts (Master the Art & Science of Living Within Your Means)

> *"Beware of little expenses. A small leak will sink a ship."*
>
> *—Ben Franklin*

Put away your credit cards! Start paying off your debts! Plug the leaks in your financial bucket! Now let's bring all those pieces together. How do you make it all work? How do you allocate money to pay a bill one month and at the same time make sure you have enough money for groceries or the utility bill? That can be a challenge. Now it's time to begin bringing together all that we have discussed previously into a unified household money management system.

I know a couple who, when they were younger, had so little money that they were constantly faced with tough choices. They used to laugh about it, saying their finances were so tight they squeaked. At the grocery store, they struggled to stay within their allotted amount, often asking the cashier to total up their bill several times during the checkout process, and sometimes having to put items back. Their snack of choice (or at least what they could afford) was popcorn, purchased unpopped (not microwave), and their big treat was two donuts and the newspaper on Sunday. They would discuss such things as, "If we put only five gallons of gas in the car today, maybe we can afford to go to the movies tonight."

That was 25 years ago. Today, because they learned to manage their money back during their salad days (or popcorn days, as they described them), their choices now are whether to spend a week on St. Maarten in the Caribbean or visit Sicily for ten days.

You can do the same. In this section, we will look at how to manage money effectively. Let's start with a simple task – paying your bills.

$$$

Pay Your Bills on Time

This may sound obvious, but the first thing to consider is the need to make sure your bills are paid on time. This should be a no-brainer, but it's not. Every month, millions of Americans miss a payment deadline, often nonchalantly, and without recognizing the damage they're doing to their financial well-being.

I have a friend who always pays her bills on time. However, one month, she missed a due-date. She wrote out the check, stamped the envelope, put the bill in her purse … and forgot about it. She discovered her oversight the day the bill was due and made a special trip to the post office. Too late. She was stunned to discover on her next notice that, while she was properly credited for the payment, her interest rate on her credit card had been increased from 18 percent, which was bad enough, to 30 percent! Most people would not have noticed, but she reviewed her bills carefully each month. She was on the phone right away to ask why her rate had jumped. The credit card representative explained that because her last payment had been late, the rate automatically went up. Company policy.

My friend pointed out that she had been a customer for well over ten years and this was the first time she had ever been late on a payment, and this "jacking up of my rate" was not acceptable. Interestingly, when she threatened to cancel her card, the representative immediately reduced the rate back to the original 18 percent. Good for her. However, what if she hadn't reviewed her invoice every month? She could have been paying that higher rate forever.

The lessons: first, never miss a payment. Second, review your bills each month. Third, fight stupid policies. Fourth, note how much discretion the companies give in terms of rates and "policies."

The real point is that if you ever think your creditors don't care about you, try missing a payment. Being a few days late on a bill does more than rile up the credit card company. Not only will they come after you with "Please remit immediately!" warnings or, worse, hike up your rate and not bother to announce it, but they will blab about your missed payment to people who can do you dirt – namely the credit bureaus. As a result, your credit rating can be damaged. You could end up not being able to borrow money. Just as bad, with a shaky credit/payment history, lenders will gleefully charge you a higher rate on future money. You don't need that kind of grief. So, pay your bills on time.

$ $ $

The Mechanics of Bill Paying

The two most common reasons bills do not get paid have nothing to do with lack of money. It is generally a matter of money management. The two most common excuses are (1) "It got lost," and (2) "I forgot."

Unpaid bills rarely have anything to do with a lack of money. More often the reason is a lack of organization. Usually, it's a matter of misplacing the invoice ("I put it on the counter. I don't know where it went.") or simply not having a system for paying bills. The problem is that unpaid bills – and bills that are paid late – can tear up your credit rating and disrupt your household's financial equilibrium. The best solution is to set up a sure-fire system for making sure bills get paid on time. So, let's do the next wealth builder.

$ $ $

Wealth Builder #19
Your Bill Payment System

The "secret" to never missing a payment or being charged late-payment fees is to have a bill payment system. To create yours, complete the next exercise in the *Back to Basics Book of Money Workbook*.

$ $ $

Uh Oh! "The Budget" Talk

You had a sneaky suspicion it was coming. You were right. So, let's have The Budget Talk!

How important is a budget? Well, my view is that you either go on a budget or go broke! People hate budgets. They whine about them, argue about them, defend to the death why budgets don't work, why budgets aren't for them ... well, you get the picture. You've probably taken a stab at drafting a household budget in the past. It's probably sitting in the junk drawer right now, another nice idea that looked great for three weeks and then was put to rest ... out of sight, out of mind.

Do You Really Need a Budget?

Multi-national corporations devote hundreds of hours and hundreds of thousands of dollars developing their budgets. The same with governments. They establish them so they know where their money goes each year. They create them so they know what they can afford to do, how many people they can afford to hire, what they can spend and what they can't. They do not create them for fun. They create them because they are necessary.

Yes, they need a budget. And so do you.

Not a Budget; A Spending Plan

Okay, first, let's change a few rules. I'm not all that fond of budgets, either, but that's mostly because the term itself is constricting and negative. Budgets are about how you cannot spend money. Actually, what we're really going to do on the following pages is develop a way to help you spend your money more effectively, based on a strategy that benefits you and makes your life easier.

I prefer to think of it as a "spending plan" rather than a budget. Either way, I know, you are already either starting to get restless, thinking that you have some better things to do right now, or getting that cold, empty feeling settling into your stomach (though it cannot be worse than the feeling of being on vacation and discovering that your credit card is over the limit). Well, hang on; what follows is really not that painful.

$ $ $

Why We Hate Budgets

We hate budgets because they do not work! Most fail – doomed from the start – because they are either too complicated or too rigid. Worse, they are generally designed with self-flagellation in mind ... a financial straight jacket that punishes us for past financial sins.

A functional budget is a flexible tool that is supposed to work *for* us; it reflects our lifestyles and interests and helps us achieve our financial goals. It's supposed to make our lives better. It works by cutting out wasteful spending, leaving us with more money for the things we really want. By setting up a simple, common sense budget, we can improve our standard of living by as much as 10 percent almost immediately.

Here are four reasons why people have problems with budgets:

1. They offer too much reality. For many people, it is easier to just go along – earning and spending and seeing how the checkbook looks at the end of the month, hoping to be pleasantly surprised.   Especially if they are not managing their money all that well, having a budget is like having a pimple on their face and being forced to spend all day looking in the mirror.

2. Setting up a budget takes a bit of work, especially if you have not done one before, or at least recently. You have to find, calculate and fiddle with a lot of numbers.

3. Many people simply do not understand them. Therefore, they hate the idea of living on a budget. They say it strangles them, enslaves them. However, nothing could be further from the truth. Mastering the discipline of living on a budget is liberating. It boosts your standard of living and your quality of life. Many couples find that working with their budget becomes a fun game on the road to financial healing, as they map out how to manage their money on a daily basis.

4. Finally – and this is the real reason most budgets fail – most of them ignore human nature. Some people – those who eschew budgets or claim they don't work – see them as a hairshirt that makes their lives miserable. And too often, the way their budgets are set up, they're right.

$ $ $

Meet Your "Household Spending Plan"

Okay, enough about what is wrong with budgets. From this page and this day forward, we will discuss your "household spending plan." And let's start thinking of it as a positive tool. Why? Because it is. A well-constructed spending plan is your valued ally that will help liberate you from financial stress and empower you to live better than ever on the money you earn. That's why setting up and following your household spending plan is a major step. It will become the cornerstone of your financial stability and growing financial security. It is how you will manage your money, establish financial balance, and bring harmony into your life.

The bottom line: you cannot live well without a spending plan. No, it is not all that much fun to set up; however, it is a flat-out necessity. And once you have it hammered into shape, you will actually love it.

A spending plan provides a systematic, proven way to manage your money and your spending. Otherwise, it's all guesswork, and your spending will reflect how full or flat your pockets feel rather than what you need and can afford. A spending plan enables you to allocate your money on short-term and long-term expenses. In the end, if you build a spending plan that works for you, you will live better – and get much more value – for the money you spend.

$ $ $

Spending Plan Guidelines

On the following pages and in your workbook, you will begin to set your spending plan down as a working document that will help you get control of your money and your life. Here are some guidelines in terms of what proportion of your money you should allocate for five major categories:

1. **Housing**: Try to spend no more than 30 percent of your take-home income on housing: rent, mortgage, insurance, and real estate taxes. This may require some changes. For example, I knew one young lady whose take-home pay was $2,500 a month. Her rent for a pretty spacious townhouse apartment for herself and her daughter came to $1,100, or 44 percent of her net income. She became a slave to her landlord, struggling to make her rent payment each month. This also impacted the rest of her life, sapping money that could have gone for groceries and other basic expenses. When she moved to an apartment that rented for $800, she immediately improved her lifestyle significantly.

2. **Savings:** Try to save at least 5 percent of your net income, more if possible. So, if you earn $3,000 a month, set aside at least $150. How do you save money out of each paycheck? The next Wealth Builder will show you.

$ $ $

Wealth Builder #20
Pay Yourself First

The "secret" (yes, another "secret") to saving money is to pay yourself first. To learn how to do just that, complete the next exercise in the *Back to Basics Book of Money Workbook*.

3. **Transportation**: The general rule of thumb is to allocate no more than 15 percent of net income for transportation. This includes car payments, insurance, license plates and registration, maintenance, parking, public transportation. Once again, if you bring home $3,000 a month, try not to spend more than $450 of that on transportation. This is the ideal. However, it can be tough if you are making two car payments. If you cannot achieve 15 percent today, just try to whittle it down over time. (Later on, you'll learn how to eliminate your care payments.)

4. **Debt:** One guideline is to allocate no more than 15 percent of net income on all (other than mortgage or rent) consumer debt: credit cards, student loans, tax debts, retail installment payments, personal loans. If your debt is out or line, though, you may need to increase that to 20 percent.

5. **Other:** This is not meant to be a catchall category, but to make it easier to segment your funds. In this "other" category, if all the above categories make sense to you, the rest of your net income – approximately 30 percent – can be used for other expenses. This will include food, clothing, entertainment, insurance, utilities, home maintenance, medical care, childcare, tuition, gifts, charity, and vacations.

Does this look tough? Here is the beauty of these five categories: they account for 100 percent of your net income. If you find that the "buckle doesn't close" when you make these calculations, keep in mind that you have the same problem – with or without a spending plan. With your spending plan, however, you can begin to whip it into shape.

$ $ $

Wealth Builder #21
Your Trial Spending Plan

It can take several attempts to get your spending plan just right. To design your first trial spending plan, complete the next exercise in the *Back to Basics Book of Money Workbook.*

$ $ $

Your Household Spending Plan

Now it's time to bite the bullet and create your actual spending plan. The key is simplicity. All you need is a legal pad or notebook, pencil and about an hour. Once again, make sure you do this together. Your spending plan will impact every aspect of your lives. It is crucial that you agree on how you allocate and spend your money.

Then follow these steps. Take your time. Expect to go through a few sheets of paper to get all your figures in sync. Establishing a spending plan requires a great deal of trial and error. That's normal, so do not become discouraged. It is like putting together a puzzle. Plus, once you have it mapped out, you will need to be adjust it periodically, as your circumstances change (if one of you gets a raise, if your rent or real estate taxes go up, etc.). For now, though, remember that this is the toughest part, but it is well worth the effort.

So take this on faith. Your spending plan will gradually make sense and begin to fit. Do not expect to get it all right the first time. The key to an effective spending plan is going through several drafts and adjusting it. Also, note that we are not providing you with a worksheet or form. This is your spending plan, so you will make your own form. Set aside several hours over several evenings to get your spending plan down on paper. Oh, and by the way, use a pencil … with an eraser. You'll see why as you get into the planning process.

$ $ $

Wealth Builder #22
Setting Up Your Spending Plan

Now it's time to establish your own spending plan. To complete this 10-step process, go to the next exercise in the *Back to Basics Book of Money Workbook*.

$ $ $

The bottom line: remind yourself that nothing beats the feeling of being able to open a bill without flinching; driving by the long lines at the bank on Friday afternoon; knowing you'll be vacationing in the Caribbean next year and not have to borrow a cent to do it; or, most of all, that your finances are in your control and working for you.

Making Your Spending Plan Work – A Dozen Hot Tips

The devil is in the details, or in the case of your spending plan, in the mechanics of executing it week after week. At this point, your spending plan must feel a bit uncomfortable, if not overwhelming. Hang tough. It will get easier.

To make your plan work smoothly, experiment with some of the following ideas that have proven effective:

1. ***Start your spending plan on Wednesday*** *of each week. This is the day you go to the bank or credit union and take out all your spending money for the week: for groceries, gas, lunches, incidentals, those sort of items. Why Wednesday? Because, for many people, the big spending days are the weekends. So, they may grocery shop on Wednesday or Thursday, but generally run errands, go to the movies, dine out and just play on Friday night, Saturday and Sunday. So, odds are that they may be pretty tight on cash by Sunday night.*

   However, the rationale behind the Wednesday start date is that they can limp along, if necessary through Monday or Tuesday with little cash in your pockets. Try it. It works. You'll be amazed how you will become accustomed to knowing exactly how much money you have in your pocket or purse at any given time and how you will begin to make dozens of mental decisions each week about how to spend that money wisely.

2. ***Segregate funds.*** *Use your checkbook to track regular, fixed expenses. For periodic expenses and special funds, set up separate accounts to warehouse cash. For example, if you pay your car insurance quarterly and the bill in $210, set up a separate account into which you will put $70 a month. (Put another slip in your bill box as a reminder.)*

   *Remember, you already have that vacation fund you set up earlier. Keep putting X dollars each month into that account. You may end up with half a dozen savings accounts. Do whatever it takes to make it work. Label them clearly and transfer funds as needed from checking to savings and then back again when the bills come in. (**Reminder:** It's a great feeling to know that when a large bill arrives you have the full amount on hand to pay it without saying, "Oh, no, how will we pay this?")*

3. **Make only one visit to the bank or credit union each week.** *Take out the full amount you have budgeted for cash expenditures (groceries, gas, entertainment, other spending, etc.) at that time. No return trips, and that includes not going to the automatic teller machine! On those visits, you should make any transfers into or out of savings accounts for various expenses. Don't expect to get it all right immediately.*

   At first, this money shuffle can seem confusing, and you may need to visit your financial institution several times a week until you get the hang of knowing when you will need to transfer funds. Most important, however, is that you do not dip into any other accounts or take out cash beyond your budget amount. (If you find that you simply cannot live on the amount you have earmarked for spending, go back and revisit and revise your spending plan.)

4. **Keep away from those credit and debit cards.** *Use them only for emergencies. Remember that paying down your debts will eventually give you more money each week. Remember also that if you cannot afford to pay cash, you cannot afford to buy it!*

5. **Leave your checkbook at home.** *Use it only to pay bills. For everything else, use the cash from your weekly budget.*

6. **Multiply weekly expenses by 4.2** *when entering them into your budget. This is the average number of weeks in a month. (Yes, February can seem like a bonus month.)*

7. **Do not borrow from one budget item** *to pay for something in another. This method of robbing from Peter to pay Paul never works.*

8. **Never write checks for money that is not in your account.** *Do what it takes to make sure the money is there.*

9. ***Prepare to make some tough decisions.*** *Example #1: If your wallet and your gas tank are both low, you may not be able to go! Example #2: You may want to have one wonderful dinner and a movie out a week. Just remember that you may end up skipping lunch or not being able to afford to buy groceries. These are your choices. You make them. You live with them.*

10. ***Test your spending plan*** *over the next few weeks and months. Remember, this document is not intended to be carved in stone. It is a living document, and it probably will end up looking a mess, with scribbled notes and adjustments, as you hammer it into shape. So, fiddle with it and make adjustments. Do NOT file it away in a drawer, which is the fate of most budgets. Keep your spending plan in the bill box and refer to it each week, when you pay your bills and plan withdrawals.*

11. ***Stick to your spending plan,*** *month after month. It will not always be easy. You will have to make choices and tell yourself "no" from time to time. But it will be worth it in the long run.*

12. ***The bonus: it will get easier.*** *That's a promise. When you first start using your spending plan, it will feel awkward and even restrictive. In the long run, however, you will find that you not only have more money for the things you truly want and need, but you will also have more freedom. So, give your spending plan time and be patient. Also remember that a spending plan is not confining. On the contrary, it is liberating, and it will enable you to live better on the money you have.*

═══════════════

What's Next: You are mastering the art and science of balancing your spending, reducing your debt, and living on your income. This involves day-to-day money management. However, what happens if an emergency comes along? The next Couple Money Skill you will learn is how to begin saving for a rainy day … and some sunshiny ones, too.

Next: Couple Money Skill #8 Stockpile a Cash Cushion

$ $ $

Couple Money Skill #8:

Stockpile a Cash Cushion
(How to Pay Cash for Emergencies,
Appliances ... Even Your Next Car!)

> *"A penny saved is a penny earned."*
> *—Ben Franklin*

How much money do you have in the bank right now? If you needed $500 in a hurry, could you go to your savings account and find it? If not, what will happen when your lawnmower takes its last gasp? When that pipe bursts and floods the bathroom? When you are driving down the highway and that clunking sound turns out to be worse than you thought?

Up to now, you are learning how to manage your money on a daily, weekly and monthly basis. You have also learned how to begin whittling down debt and living on cash. Now let's look a bit ahead. Unfortunately, life does not always take your spending plan into consideration. Life hurls screaming knuckleballs at you every now and then, and it seems that when one comes at you, the batting machine picks up speed and they come in fast and furious rapid succession. That's why it's now time to add another layer of security to your strategy for financial peace.

Be Prepared

Howard and Deb are good money managers. Among the many things they do right – and that keep their finances and their relationship from being tossed and buffeted by every unexpected expense that pops up – is that they put aside just $50 each month into a special savings account they labeled their "Emergency Fund."

That may seem like a small amount (just $1.66 per day), but the results are huge. Not only does it add up to $600 in a year (plus some interest), but it keeps many unexpected expenses from becoming crises that might otherwise disrupt their monthly spending plan.

Over the years, the amount in their "Emergency Fund" account has ebbed and flowed, risen and fallen, as an appliance needed replacing one month or the garage door needed fixing another; or when they had to replace their son's stolen gym bag, along with his expensive running shoes. These little setbacks might have upset their spending plan. However, because of their Emergency Fund, they didn't miss a beat. That's one small component in the plan that has led them to ongoing financial peace and stability.

Here's the premise of this chapter: you need a cash cushion under your financial butt that allows you to take minor emergencies on the chin without sending your budget and overall financial stability to the matt for the count. Plus, you need to start thinking about how you are going to buy big-ticket items – from dishwashers to new furnaces to vacation trips – with cash.

Actually, it's quite simple. Start squirreling money away for a rainy day. Do not do this every now and then, hit or miss, but as part of a plan and strategy. You should already have at least one savings account, probably three or four. Well, you will end up with a few more by the end of this chapter.

That's because, as you save money for specific needs and purposes, you will be able to…

- Pay for emergencies and other unpleasant and unexpected expenses with cash … and with a smile on your face.

- Pay cash for that next appliance, vacation, sunroom addition, and even your next car.

- Sleep like a baby at night because you know you have your "what-ifs" covered.

$ $ $

The Problem with Saving Money

Here's the catch: saving money can be tricky. No, it's actually not hard to do, once you get the hang of it. But getting started can be a bear. Still, learn how to do it right, and your financial life will become much more stable … and in turn your personal life much more peaceful.

Money in the Bank

Scenario #1:

"Well, Honey, we had no choice. We needed a new hot water heater. The old one finally quit. We knew it was on its last legs."

"But that's $858 to buy a new one, have it installed and have the old one carted away? We're not made of money, you know."

"Don't yell at me. The old one quit. We had no time to shop around. Do you want the kids to shower in cold water?"

"Fine. Well, it's not my fault, either, you know. Well, happy anniversary. That great weekend away we'd planned? The money just went for a new hot water heater."

Scenario #2:

"Darn. Well, we knew the old water heater was about to go."

"And it just did. Here's the bill for $858."

"Whew. A lot of money. How much did we have in the emergency account?"

"A little over $800. I already went online and shifted what we had in the emergency account into our main checking. The bill's paid. We'll be a little short this week, but we had to have the new heater."

"Could have been worse. What time to do you want to head out tomorrow for our anniversary weekend?"

"Let's say after three. Oh, Honey, that will be so much fun."

―――――――――

Which scenario do you want when the next minor emergency comes along? All you have to do is start planning ahead. Sure, it's not often possible to predict when a financial emergency will occur. Perhaps it's a minor crisis, such as a failed hot water heater in your house or a new screen door. Or it may be something much more serious, such as a long-term illness or disability. (For these latter ones, that's where insurance comes into play, which we'll talk about in the next chapter.)

So, while it is often not possible to predict when financial emergencies will occur. However, that does not mean it is impossible to prepare for them in advance. On the contrary, you can. That's because they *will* occur. That is almost a guarantee. People who are financially solid and at peace in their relationship do not have fewer financial problems. They are simply better prepared for them.

No, it is not necessary to know the particulars. That doesn't matter. What does matter is having the money available when it is needed. However, that may be easier said than done. The real problem is that it is hard to save money. Most people mean to save. The idea of putting money aside makes sense. Unfortunately, many people simply never get around to doing it. Part of the problem is that money can be tight. They are busy raising children, paying for a home, taking that well-deserved vacation now and then. Every month, they may promise themselves that, after the bills are paid *this* month, they will "send ahead" whatever is left. And they have every intention of doing just that, but....

That's the point: there's always a "but ..." In the end, more often than not, there is nothing left at the end of the month. Something always seems to come up: that once-minor drip in the downstairs bathroom gets too persistent to ignore (plumber: $175); the carpets can't go another month without cleaning (steam cleaning: $375); that little thumping sound below your feet in the car turns out to be the transmission getting ready to head south (big bucks); that late-night trip to the ER, though it proves to be only indigestion, still rings up a ton of non-covered medical bills under your deductible (bigger bucks).

Plus, it's not always about emergencies. There's that 50 percent off on a fabulous vacation ... that still costs the other 50 percent. Or, how about that just-gotta-have outfit or power tool? Or then there's the realization that it's April 8th, and you just remembered that your anniversary is April 9th. The list goes on. These little financial setbacks are hard to factor into your spending plan. So, whether it is to manage emergencies or save for everything from a new car to the year-end holiday expenses, smart money managers incorporate a savings plan into their spending plan. They set up a systematic savings plan, one that regularly takes money out of the spending loop and puts it into a safe stash.

$ $ $

Set Up Your Cash Cushion for Emergencies

The first step is to build an emergency fund. This is really so easy you won't believe it. All you have to do is add one more item to your written spending plan and then take that pay-yourself-first money out of your hands and deposit it into a separate account at your financial institution. The goal is to begin building a cash cushion to meet out-of-the-ordinary expenses that might otherwise disrupt your spending plan.

The rule of thumb is that you should accumulate an amount equal to at least three months' income. Six is even better. However, the actual amount is not as important as the process that steadily sets aside X dollars each month. You will need to study your spending plan, scratch your heads a bit and determine an amount that you both agree you can reasonably afford to set aside each month. Perhaps it is $100. Can you do that? If so, after a year (barring the need to tap the funds for an emergency) you will have $1,200 on hand, plus interest. Imagine the feeling that you can take a $1,200 hit and not end up scrambling to find money to pay that bill. What a great feeling! The amount isn't all that crucial. The important thing is to keep building that fund ... month after month after month. So, let's do it now.

$ $ $

Wealth Builder #23
Create Your "Emergency Fund"

The goal is to create a cash cushion to help you weather emergencies. To do this, go to the next exercise located in the *Back to Basics Book of Money Workbook*.

$ $ $

Saving for Big-Ticket Items

Now let's look at your next saving venture. Emergencies are unplanned expenses. However, you can also save for planned purchases: vacations, boats, even cars. So, let's look at how to save for big-ticket items. But first, why? Well, remember that we are weaning ourselves off debt. If you save for your next big purchase, you will stay off the financial treadmill of always living a year or two behind on the money you spend. With your emergency fund, you can fix and replace most items. What about a trip to Europe or a new car? Why not save for it? It is always better to earn interest to than pay it!

The concept is simple. Let's say you want to buy a boat or take a cruise. For the sake of simplicity, let's also say the cost will be $5,000. You'd love to have it today. However, you know that it makes more sense to wait and save up for it. So, you target 24 months. Do the math. How much must you put aside each month, ignoring earned interest, to have $5,000 in 24 months? $208.33. Not bad. And if you can pay cash for it, you may even get as much as 10 percent off, so you then have an extra $500.

If that seems like a lot of money, keep in mind that this is money you would have to pay either way – whether you saved for it or borrowed on a credit card. So, the real choice is do you want to pay yourself interest or pay it to a lender?

Now, remember that fun fund you set up at the beginning of this book? You planned a getaway or the purchase of something outside your spending plan. That will become your long-term fund for a particular purpose. I recommend setting up separate accounts for each specific goal. Open the account and tape the name and purpose on the front, and put that pay-to-yourself bill in your bill box.

What else do you want...and can afford? A vacation of a lifetime? A redesigned kitchen? A new jet ski or snowmobile? (We'll look at such long-term topics as college funding for your children and retirement planning in a later chapter. For now, we are exploring more immediate items, those that we hope to achieve within a year or two or three.) Set your sights carefully. Remember, you work hard for your money, so choose carefully what you want to spend it on. Also, don't go hog wild. Learn to prioritize your goals. You will probably not be able to afford everything you want. Focus on one or two key dreams.

$ $ $

Wealth Builder #24
Setting Up Special Funds

You can begin saving money for your short-term and long-term dreams. To learn how to begin setting up special funds, complete the next exercise in the *Back to Basics Book of Money Workbook*.

$ $ $

How to Pay Cash for Your Next Car

Yes, you can even buy your next car with cash. And we will devote the remainder of this chapter to this important topic. But first, why a special section devoted solely to buying cars? The answer is that Americans love cars, and all too often we put our brains on cruise control when we buy them. If we don't love them big, with wide tires and running boards, we love them sleek and trim and safe enough to boast a "Baby on Board" window sticker. Or we love them bio-friendly, and are willing to spend a fortune in order to cut our fuel costs or get a government credit on our taxes. Whether we like to admit it or not, we think of our vehicles as extensions of ourselves, of our personalities. We love them and we pay good money for them, almost always on credit. In fact, most of us have not been without a car payment since our first vehicle.

Most of all, for most of us, our cars are the second biggest purchase we make, right behind our homes. Every month, the two payments that always show up month after month, after month are the mortgage and the car payment. When it comes to our vehicles, what we buy, what we pay, and how long we keep them become major factors in our financial stability and peace of mind. That's right. The vehicles we buy and the money we pay for them play a major role in our quality of life … not just behind the wheel, but on the domestic front, as well.

Men & Women & Cars

Men and women see cars differently. Never were Mars and Venus further from each other. Women are guilty of buying the wrong cars for the wrong reasons. And men are even guiltier! Both sexes are nuts in their own ways when it comes to their driving machines.

Men and women both tend to switch off their brains when it comes to buying cars, although they hit different buttons. Both ignore the big question of value. For example, a woman (and I know, I risk being drawn and quartered for making such big-swatch generalities) will tend to focus on color and amenities – from heated seats to power sliding doors and built-in DVD players for the kids – and safety. Still, a woman also tends to keep a car longer than a man would. She leans toward a vehicle that is reasonable in terms of features, and then she bonds with it. Almost every woman I've known who had purchased her own car fell in love with it and was surprised when it began to click past the 100,000 mile point and a man recommended that she begin looking for a new vehicle. When it finally died or just became too expensive to repair, she would go through a brief mourning period and then, reluctantly, replace it.

Guys, on the other hand, are borderline (if not over-the-edge) irrational when it comes to cars. I'm no exception. In fact, I'm getting all excited as I write this chapter. I see a hot, low-slung vehicle that spellbinds me, refer to it as "sex on wheels" and can just imagine tearing down the highway in it, or putting it through its paces on a winding country road, downshifting as it slides through those tight turns. Even the most sane and rational of men goes through major mind-blown angst, balancing practicality with sex appeal, as we wrestle over whether or not to buy that dream car … with no guarantee that practicality will even come in a close second.

The bottom line of all this is that some women and many men (once again, don't hang me for the gross generalization) lose all rational powers of thinking when it comes to cars. As a result, they risk wasting thousands of dollars on their vehicles. That's money that could go toward any number of better uses.

Just as bad, many men and women have grown to accept lifelong car payments! Here's a story worth repeating: years ago, during my salad days, I knew a co-worker who learned that I had just paid off my first new-car loan. I was proud and bragging about it. To me, this four-year old car was now mine, and I was free of the monthly payment. This was money in my pocket each month, money I could use to enhance the quality of my young family's life. But when I told my co-worker about making the last payment, he got all excited and asked what car I was going to buy next. I was a bit confused at first. When I told him I wasn't planning to buy anything for awhile, that the vehicle was only four years old and in good shape, that I could use that $168 a month (yes, it was some years ago) in any number of ways to raise my young family's standard of living, and, besides, I planned to "drive it 'til the wheels fell off," it was his turn to be confused. He informed me that I was wasting all that credit I could be using. "You could have a brand new car," he told me, incredulous that I could be so stupid not to rush out and buy it right away. That was the day I realized many people had a very cockeyed view of the world and their money, especially when it came to their cars.

Need more evidence that lunacy rules the lives of many of us when it comes to our cars? Another friend lamented to me that he would have to put off buying his first home because, a car lover, he had made a number of bad decisions. He had traded three cars in the last two years, as he kept falling in love with yet another bright and shiny toy. As fate would have it, he managed to buy his cars brand new and sell them right at the point where the value had begun to plunge. He was in debt up to his eyeballs. I know another fellow who drove one of those urban tanks, so big you just about had to climb into it with a ladder. And he traded it every year for a new one. When he went broke, he got some small satisfaction out of recognizing that he was driving to the poor house in one hot set of wheels.

$ $ $

Some Sanity on Buying Cars

Men and women, I invite you to forget about what you know, think and believe about cars. Here are some facts to bring you to sanity and common ground together:

1. **Cars aren't toys.** I'm not talking about the hobbyist or collector. Even then, those are investments. For most of us, however, our cars are vehicles. They are transportation. Yes, we want them to be attractive and reliable and sometimes even sexy. But they're not toys, and if we can afford to throw money away on endless car payments, we still could find better use for that $300 or $400 or $500 or even bigger check we write each month.

2. **Today's cars are designed to go 200,000 miles** with little trouble. Car manufacturers have mastered the workings of the internal combustion engine and all the computerized gizmos that go into them. Where 40 years ago or so we needed to keep a tool box in the trunk and have at least a basic working knowledge of the vehicles we drove, today's cars are built so all we have to do is turn the key, hit the gas and go, changing the oil every 3,000 miles or so, and that's about it. So, if you drive 15,000 a year, your car can give you good service for more than a decade. And then you can give it to your son or daughter, and get a few more years of use out of it after that.

3. **Leasing is for dummies** (and for some, but not all, business owners). It's a good deal for everyone but you. The dealer gets to sell you a car and then get it back in three years. It used to be that you could lease a car for no money down. Even that is no longer true. Today, you buy your car for no money down, but you have to kick in a few thousand dollars when you lease. (Paying a lump sum in advance to reduce your monthly payments makes no sense.) Imagine shelling out $3,500 at signing, making $347 payments for three years and then handing a practically new car back to the dealership. Plus, you have

to pay for insurance, sometimes for the routine maintenance, and always for any miles you drive over your contract limit. It makes no sense to fork over thousands of dollars and have nothing to show for it in the end. Saying leasing is smart is like saying that you'd be better off renting a home versus buying it. The only exception: if you're a business owner and want to deduct 100 percent of your vehicle's cost each year. Even then, work out the numbers before you sign a lease.

Instead, why not buy your next car outright, drive it for 10 years (an arbitrary number, but good enough for most purposes), and then pay CASH for your next vehicle?

$ $ $

Step by Step: How to Pay Cash for Your Next Car

Here is how to get your ducks in a row and buy your next car for cash. The following assumes that you are in the market for a new car today and that you have not set aside any money for the purchase:

1. **Pick your car wisely.** You want quality, style, reliability… and yes, something that makes your soul soar. But buy it for the long term. Plan to own it for 10 to 12 years. Get out the buyer's guides. (If you plan to do only limited research, use the *Consumer Reports* car ratings guide.) Consider insurance costs: some cars are discounted for safety; others receive add-on surcharges. Then go window shopping, getting to know a few salespeople at dealerships and test-driving several cars. However, do not commit at this point. Just look, touch, drive and research.

Does your auto insurer give a safety discount?

Or maybe you will be penalized for driving that super-fast blue-streak sports car. Before you buy your next car, find out how it is ranked for safety by The Insurance Institute for Highway Safety.

Visit www.iihs.org for more information.

---

2. **Buy nearly-new, not new.** Most vehicles drop anywhere from 20 percent to 30 percent in value the second they leave the dealer showroom. I routinely find it is possible to buy a one-year-old vehicle with around 10,000 miles for as much as 35 percent off the original price. Plus, it still has most of the new-car warranty.

3. **Shop around and negotiate the best price.** The auto industry is super competitive these days. As a rule of thumb, go to at least three dealerships before making your final decision. Deal hard.

4. **Look for the best financing deal.** Remember, we are assuming you do not have any cash set aside for this care, so you want to cut the best deal for your money. That includes financing. But be skeptical about those "$2,000 off or 1.4 percent" financing deals. Such either-or deals put no money back in your pocket in the long run. Ask for both! Unless the deal is terrific, consider using a home equity line of credit. The rate is usually competitive, and the interest is tax deductible. Just remember that when you use your home equity, you are also placing your home as the collateral for your car.

> **You may be in line for a break on your auto insurance when you turn 50 or 55.** Insurers know that this is the safest group, with the best safety record. Talk to your insurer.
> **Caution:** Rates often go up again when you hit 70.

5. **Go for the shortest financing term you can afford.** Obtaining financing for six years can put you "upside down" on your loan (owing more on the car after a few years than it is worth), and you risk paying a fortune in interest. Rule of thumb: four years. That is generally short enough so that you can save on interest payments, but not so short that your monthly payments are overwhelming.

6. **Keep making car payments after the car is paid off.** After four years, your car is paid off and still in good shape. Depending on how many miles you drive it each year, it may have between six and eight good years left in it. For the sake of discussion, let's say six years. Let's also say you have been paying $500 each month. So, what do you do with that $500 you were paying to the bank, credit union or car finance people? Every month, keep making that $500 payment, but this time to yourself.

   Remember, the idea is to be able to pay cash for your NEXT car. Open up an account and either write a check every month or have automatic transfers made into your "new car" account. After six years, you will have a 10-year-old car for a trade-in, to keep for your kids or just to keep on driving. Plus, you will have $36,000 saved. Plus, if you earn 4 percent on average on your money, you will have more than $41,200 for your next vehicle.

7. **Pay cash for your next car.** When the time comes to buy your next car, you won't pay any interest. You've been earning it, rather than paying it. Plus, you can walk into a dealership, find the next car of your dreams and make a simple offer: "I want to buy this car, for this price, with cash, today!" You will get a great deal on the car you want. And if they offer you a terrific financing deal you can't refuse, you will have $40,000 plus for other uses. Congratulations!

What's Next: You are mastering the art and science of balancing your spending, reducing your debt, and living well on your income. And now you are learning the art and science of saving money for emergencies and big-ticket items. By now you should have several savings accounts or separate accounts set up. Make sure you continue to fund them according to your spending plan strategy. You are becoming proficient in day-to-day money management, as well as long-term planning. Plus, you are starting to build wealth and assets. You even have money for minor emergencies.

However, what happens if a big emergency comes along? The next Couple Money Skill you will learn is how to protect your assets.

Next: Couple Money Skill #9 Protect Your Assets

$ $ $

Couple Money Skill #9

Protect Your Assets
(Use Insurance to Turn Mountains into Mole Hills!)

> *"Insurance: The Widow's Friend."*
>
> *— Sign on an Agent's Desk*

You're working hard, knocking down debt and building financial strength. Admit it, there are times (okay, perhaps just moments) when you are having fun, enjoying managing and being in control of your financial life. And you're doing it together, as a couple. If all is going according to plan, you are building financial strength and relationship strength.

So, now let's talk about how to protect what you have achieved so far and what you will achieve in the future. This money-skill section is about protecting and preserving not just your assets, but also your value as a generator of income and wealth. This section is about insurance. No, don't roll your eyes. It's an important subject. You don't want to work like a dog to rebuild your financial stability, only to watch it get swept away in an instant by a slippery spot on the road, a destructive storm, a misplaced foot on the top step of the stairs.

Here's the premise: if nothing big ever goes wrong, you don't need insurance. But homes burn down, breadwinners die, spouses become disabled, cars get in accidents, and neighbors' children fall out of tree houses. Any one of these events can destroy financial stability. That's why there's insurance. It's really a pretty good deal. Literally, for pennies on the dollar, you can help assure that an asset worth upwards of hundreds of thousands of dollars is replaced, repaired or rebuilt.

For example, imagine paying, say, $500 a year for disability insurance with a monthly benefit of $2,000. (By the way, these figures are for illustration purposes only.) You pay this premium for ten years and are never sick a day. You've shelled out $5,000! What a waste! No, not really. Not at all. Because, then one day it happens: some drunk driver crosses the center line; some nasty virus makes you too weak to go to work; for whatever reason, your health takes a serious tumble, and you find yourself totally and permanently disabled … and your income along with you. But then those disability checks start to arrive, month after month. $2,000 a month! Ah ha! All makes sense now. And here's the real kicker: you have recouped your total premium costs in two and a half months. If you are laid up for two years, you will receive $48,000. For pennies on the dollar, you have reduced your financial loss from "total disaster" to "inconvenient."

That's one example of why insurance is so important. So, load up on it! If you want to cut corners on your spending plan, let the roof on your house go one extra year before replacement, or borrow DVDs from the library rather than rent them on pay-per-view. Insurance is one of those things that, if you are lucky, you never need to use, but if you do, be grateful you have it.

$ $ $

Insurance Is One of the Smartest Buys

Now, a number of my clients are life insurance companies. I help them market their products and train their agents. I do it because I believe in the concept of insurance.

I've also witnessed first hand how life insurance has saved one young mother and her children from possible poverty because she and her husband had the good sense to buy life insurance. He was an attorney, rich in potential, ready to make partner in his firm. He was earning close to $150,000 a year. They had two children and had just built their dream home. They had it made, at least until he died at age 37 in a car crash.

Nothing could ease the emotional pain and suffering his widow and children went through. However, she did not have to worry about finances. Several years earlier, when their first son was born, they purchased $2,000,000 of life insurance on him and $1,000,000 on her. A month after he was killed, she received the first of what will be a lifetime of checks. She was able to keep their home, where she is raising her sons. She has money for their college educations, can return to work when she is ready (not because she is desperate for money), and will likely be able to retire (also when she is ready) in reasonable comfort.

In my own life, over the years I've had a few car accidents, endured the financial and emotional trauma of having my home burglarized, and watched my parents' house be destroyed in a fire. When my cars were damaged, I paid a few hundred bucks as my deductible; the insurance company paid the rest, one time writing checks to cover more than $13,000 in damage to a car my daughter was driving. When my home was broken into, I paid $250 in deductible, and the insurance company paid well over $3,000 to replace jewelry, electronic equipment and other items. When my parents' home caught fire, it was totally rebuilt. The total cost came to more than $170,000. They paid less than $3,000 (most of that because my mother decided it was a good time to upgrade the carpeting).

The bottom line: insurance is a good deal. Correction: insurance is a great deal. Still, every once in a while I run into some knuckleheads who cannot comprehend the concept of insurance, and who think the insurance companies are ripping them off. Yet when they get in an accident, they call the insurance company and – poof, as if by magic, it would seem – get a check in the mail in three days; when they get sick, they often don't even see the bill; it goes right to the insurance company, which sends the payment directly to the medical clinic or hospital. When they have a fire in their home, the insurer pays upwards of hundreds of thousands of dollars to have it rebuilt or restored. And when they die, their widow or widower gets a check for hundreds of thousands – sometimes even millions – of dollars. Yet, there are still people out there who think that insurance is a rip-off.

Why do some people have concerns about insurance and insurance companies? Somewhere, some people have the impression that they are supposed to make a *profit* on insurance, like with a lottery ticket. They do not understand that the purpose of insurance is to *restore* insureds to their original position, or as close to it as possible. So, if your house worth $200,000 burns to the ground, based on the terms of the contract, the insurance company will pay to have it rebuilt. They may even pay for your family to stay in a hotel while the work is being done. Yes, you may have some out-of-pocket costs. Still, let's say your annual homeowners' insurance premiums come to a thousand dollars, and you haven't had any troubles for 20 years. You can resent the fact that you have paid $20,000 over 20 years, or you can jump for joy to realize that, when the smoke hit the shingles, you got your home rebuilt for next to nothing, the equivalent of a one thousand percent return on your premium dollars.

So, get your head on straight about insurance. It's pretty important. Most of all, it's not a luxury. It's a flat-out necessity, at least if you are serious about protecting your financial stability. If you get a kick out of gambling, fine. Then just put down this book and go to the casino. However, if you care about your loved ones and want to build a financially solid lifestyle, make sure you have adequate insurance.

Remember, you are reading this book because you want to straighten out your financial life. You want to get off the financial treadmill and on the pleasant, tree-lined road to financial peace and stability. As I've been saying – and it's well worth repeating – one of the reasons you own insurance is because it protects what you work so hard to achieve. Most states have laws requiring you to have auto insurance. Also, no lender will sell you a mortgage without proof of insurance. Yes, own insurance because, by law, you *must*. But most of all, own it because you *can*.

Do not try to scrape by with the bare minimum on your car insurance, for example. If necessary, increase your deductible to keep your premium under control. But buy the best coverage you can, and as much as you reasonably need.

Most of all, you'd be nuts to consider going bare. Insurance can be your best friend. Take advantage of it. Without insurance, you and your family are vulnerable to financial disaster. This makes sense for your car and your home. But it makes just as much sense in other areas, too. Do not neglect other important insurance coverages. You need to be protected by…

- Life Insurance
- Medical Insurance
- Homeowners Insurance
- Auto Insurance
- Disability
- Personal Liability Umbrella Insurance

So, here's a mini-primer on the fundamentals you need to know about these types of coverage.

$$$

Life Insurance Protects Your Most Valuable Asset

You are worth more than you think. I'll prove it to you by looking at your most valuable asset. What is that? If you said your house or your car or your investments, you'd be wrong. Your most valuable asset is YOU. More to the point, it is your income-earning potential, sometimes referred to as your *Human Life Value*. Your Human Life Value is based on the concept that, in many respects, you are a money machine. Not very flattering, perhaps, but nonetheless true. Each week, each month, year after year, it is the income produced as a direct result of your work that keeps the economic wheels of your household turning smoothly.

But this is why life insurance is so important. It's not your job that assures you earn an income. It is your ability to work at that job to generate an income. Your income guarantees that the bills are paid, college tuitions provided, your family's lifestyle maintained ... that, each and every month, the money is in the checking account to pay the mortgage, auto and other loans, buy clothes and put food on the table.

So, what are you worth? Let's find out by looking at *your* Human Life Value. Here is a simplified rule-of-thumb way to measure how much you are worth as a "money machine" to your family: multiply your present annual income by the number of years until you plan to retire. **Example:** If you are 38, expect to retire at 65, and have a current annual income of $65,000, your Human Life Value is $1,755,000 ($65,000 X 27 years to retirement). How about that? $1.755 million!

Plus, keep in mind that this is your MINIMUM financial value. It does not factor in (1) inflation or (2) real dollar increases in your income over time. So, your actual value is probably a great deal higher! Still, this amount does give you some idea just how much you are worth to your family. So, don't ever tell anyone you are worth more dead than alive. You are more than likely worth a lot of money.

$ $ $

Wealth Builder #25
Your Human Life Value

What are you worth as a money-making asset to your family? To find out, go to and complete the next exercise in the *Back to Basics Book of Money Workbook*.

$ $ $

The Economic Value of a Stay-at-Home Parent

So, if you generate an income, you're worth a fair amount of money. But what if you stay at home, raise the kinds, cook the meals, do the laundry, keep the house clean, run somewhere between 500 and 10,000 errands every day? Well, you might be amazed just how much you are worth, as well.

The most comprehensive study to date comes from joint research conducted by University of Utah and Cornell University. The numbers differ little by income, but do vary somewhat by ethnic and marital status. But when all is said and done, the annual value of household work from married couple households comes to $20,724, regardless of the number of children.[10]

That may not sound like much. However, when it comes to raising a child from birth to age 18, this number translates into a total value of nearly $375,000.

---

[10] "Estimates of Mean Annual Value of Housework Done by Adults in the United States in 2003," University of Utah and Cornell University.

Total Cost to Raise a Child to Age 18

Age of Youngest Child	Total Value
0	$373,032
1	$352,308
2	$331,584
3	$310,860
4	$290,136
5	$269,412
6	$248,688
7	$227,964
8	$207,240
9	$186,516
10	$165,792
11	$145,068
12	$124,344
13	$103,620
14	$ 82,896
15	$ 62,172
16	$ 41,448
17	$ 20,724

So, if you have a 10-year-old child, the total estimated cost of caring for that one child for the next eight years (to age 18) will be approximately $165,792 ($20,724 X 8). However, if you have a newborn, a six-year-old, and a 10-year-old, you should still base your calculations on the age of the youngest. This is the "replacement" cost if the stay-at-home parent should die. (**Note:** As mentioned above, the cost is not generally impacted greatly by the number of children.)

The bottom line: if you or your spouse stays home for hands-on child rearing, it is important to protect the family with adequate life insurance. If that parent dies, the family's entire standard of living can be jeopardized. With adequate life insurance, however, money can be made available to provide such services as daycare, housekeeping, and more.

$ $ $

Wealth Builder #26
Stay-at-Home Parent:
What Is *Your* Economic Value?

If one of you is a stay-at-home parent, let's find out your economic value by completing the next exercise in the *Back to Basics Book of Money Workbook.*

$ $ $

The Bottom Line on Life Insurance

These human life value calculations are just estimates. But they will give you some idea how financially important you are to your family. Most of all, if something happened to you, what would happen to them? And what would happen to all that you and your partner have worked for? That is why people purchase life insurance. So, do not be penny wise and dollar foolish. Take steps to protect your most valuable asset.

$ $ $

Other Insurance

I am not going to run on for page after page about the importance of other coverage. However, I believe it is important to mention them.

Medical Insurance

Getting adequate, affordable medical coverage is a growing problem for more and more people these days. The cost of health care has gone through the roof. In fact, it has risen (and continues to rise) so fast that I will not even attempt to summarize the costs. You know health care is expensive.

If you are paying for your own coverage, you know that the cost can be prohibitive. Still, the only thing more expensive than paying big bucks for health insurance coverage is not having the coverage when you need it. A significant number of bankruptcies and home foreclosures are the result of people attempting to pay off huge medical bills.

Recommendations: First of all, you must have medical coverage. The cost may be horrendous, but the cost of going bare can be even worse. If you decide to take your chances, you are rolling the dice and hoping that you do not get sick, hoping that you do not get injured, hoping that you do not get into an accident. The whole point of managing your money and taking charge of your financial life is to remove or reduce as much as possible the element of luck and wishful thinking. I've seen people who put off necessary medical care because they could not afford it. In the end, they compounded their health problems. That is no way to live.

If you are not covered by medical insurance through work or if you are paying for all or a portion of your coverage...

1. Hang onto any coverage you presently do have. Yes, costs will continue to increase each year. If at all possible, however, keep your coverage in force.

2. Review your coverage. Do you really want to have comprehensive medical care that covers every doctor's visit and prescription? Can you afford to cover some of these expenses out of pocket? Is there a plan better suited to your needs, with a lower premium?

3. Consider a bigger deductible. Deductibles as high as $2,000 a year are not unrealistic these days. Remember, the higher your deductible, the lower your premium. Try to balance what you can reasonably afford to pay out of your own pocket with potential premium savings. The thinking is that you can raise your deductible to what you can afford to absorb each year, keeping your insurance for a major medical event. By and large, however, if you have young children, you may need to keep your deductible a bit lower.

4. Consider a health savings account (HSA), which allows you to make tax-deductible contributions. The plan is then linked to a high-deductible medical insurance plan. The premiums for the insurance tend to be about 25 percent those of traditional insurance packages. For the right people in the right circumstances, an HSA can be very effective. (I know one man who went to an HSA. His deductible was $5,000, after which pretty much all costs were covered. Additionally, he put a little over $230 a month into his HSA account, and was able to deduct the amount. He paid routine medical expenses up to his deductible from the HSA account. He reduced his health insurance premiums from more than $5,500 to under $2,000 a year.)

5. Consider changing jobs to an employer that offers health insurance. As sad as that may sound, I know of more and more families where at least one of them either took a job for the health care package or stayed at a job they would have otherwise left.

If you own a home, make sure your coverage is neither too extravagant (covering mink furs and jewelry you do not own) nor too lean (not able to cover the cost of replacing your home if it is destroyed). Also, some policies automatically increase the coverage amount and the premium every year for projected inflation. Over time, you may end up with coverage that is either too little (if inflation increases faster) or too much (if the automatic increases exceed the rate of increases in housing costs in your area). Review your coverage annually.

If you do not own your home, make sure you have renters insurance. It is usually downright cheap, and it covers your property in your apartment.

═══════════

Ten Good Reasons to Review Your Homeowners Insurance Today!

If you are like most people, your home is not just your most valuable possession and biggest asset, but it is also your family's shelter. If anything should happen to your home, you want to be sure losses will be repaired or replaced without unexpected financial surprises. That's why you carry homeowner's insurance.

That's also why it is critically important that your homeowner's coverage be current with your needs and the value of your home and its contents. You may need to increase your coverage. There is also a possibility you can reduce it ... along with your premiums.

So, now is as good a time as any to review your insurance. Here are ten good reasons:

1. *You want to make sure that new family computer is covered, along with any other electronic gizmos you've purchased recently. They may be protected, but it costs nothing to talk to your agent just to make sure. The same goes for other new items, such as jewelry, new dining room furniture, etc. Find out if you need additional coverage.*

2. *You don't want to waste money insuring items you no longer own or have in your possession. If you gave your grandmother's diamond ring to your daughter, or sold your first-edition book collection, you may be eligible for a premium reduction.*

3. *Safety pays. You may be in line for discounts if you have added safety devices. Even something as simple as installing deadbolts may reduce your costs. The same goes for burglar alarms, as well as carbon monoxide and smoke detectors. Tell your agent.*

4. *There is a good chance your home's replacement value has increased, even if its market value has declined in recent years. So, make sure your coverage is adequate to cover a full replacement in the event of a total loss. Otherwise, if you had a loss, your out-of-pocket expenses could make your homeowner's insurance premiums look like small change.*

5. *It's never a bad idea to review your deductible. A few years ago, a lower deductible might have made sense to you. However, today, if you can afford to cover more expenses yourself in a loss, you may be able to reduce your premium by increasing your deductible.*

6. *If you're getting older, your premiums could be getting better. If you're 55 or older, senior discounts at motels and restaurants aren't the only perks. You could be eligible for a discount on your homeowner's premiums. Find out. Talk to your agent.*

7. *Don't assume your policy's cost-of-living provision matches your needs. Automatic increases protect you from unexpected surprises. However, they are not tailored to your individual situation. It often requires a look at your actual policy and home value to determine if you need additional coverage or a reduction.*

8. *Make sure you're not insuring dirt. Your home's value includes the land under it, which should not be insured. Check your policy to be sure only buildings and personal property are covered.*

9. *Don't cut corners on home-business assets. More and more people today are turning that spare bedroom into an office. If you're self-employed, even part time, your business assets may not be covered under your homeowner's policy. Consider a business rider.*

10. *If a year has passed since you last reviewed your coverage, regardless of other factors, it just makes sense to meet with your Chase Insurance Agent and go over your policy. There is no cost for this review. It might even lead to a reduction in your premiums.*

Auto Insurance

If you own a car, you need auto insurance. Not only will it protect your investment in your vehicle, but it also will protect you if another driver sues you. Make sure you have the right coverage, and that you get it for the right price.

Also, keep in mind that there is a lot you can do to control your rates. Here are some suggestions:

1. **Up your deductible.** Your deductible (the amount you pay out-of-pocket when there is a claim) can be as low as $50 or as high as $1,000. The higher your deductible, the lower your premium will be. Decide how much out-of-pocket expense you can handle reasonably. Then find out how much you can save by increasing your deductible.

2. **Buy the right car.** Many sporty, high-performance models are considered high risk because they are more dangerous or more likely to be stolen. If you own one of those autos, your premium could be several times higher than what it might cost to insure a more sedate sedan. Some cars are also more expensive than others to repair. That is one reason many people call their insurance agent before they buy.

3. **Don't cut too many corners.** Some people discontinue collision coverage once the car is a certain age. However, many of today's cars are holding their value longer ... while the cost of carrying collision a few extra years may only be a few dollars.

4. **Get all the discounts** to which you are entitled. Ask about:

    • Multi-car discounts for insuring several vehicles with the same carrier. It pays to work with only one company.

    • Multi-policy discounts for insuring your home, autos, etc. with one company.

    • Good driver discounts if you have had no accidents or moving violations for a certain period of time.

- Low-mileage discounts if you drive a limited number of miles. If you use your car only to go to the grocery store once a week, you may pay a lower rate than the person who drives cross country regularly and puts on 80,000 miles a year.

- Teen-driver discounts. Your rates can soar when teenagers get behind the wheel. However, you may benefit from a good student discount if your teen maintains a certain grade point average; completes a driver training course; or is away at school at least 100 miles from home (and the car stays behind).

- Senior discounts. You may be in line for a break on your auto insurance when you turn 50 or 55. Insurers know that this is the safest group, with the best safety record. Talk to your insurer. **Caution:** Rates sometimes go up again when you hit 70.

Disability Insurance

Disability is sometimes thought of (or actually, not thought of) as the "forgotten need." We overlook it. We assume it will never happen. I'll let the statistics speak for themselves:

- More than 40 million Americans are considered disabled. (American Medical Association, 2007.)

- A person suffers a disabling work injury every nine seconds. (National Safety Council - Injury Facts 2004 Edition.)

- Almost 3 in 10 workers entering the work force today will become disabled before retiring. (Social Security Administration, Fact Sheet, January 31, 2007.)

- Forty-three percent of all 40-year olds will suffer a disability for at least 90 days prior to age 65. (2007 Field Guide to Estate Planning)

- Disability causes nearly 50 percent of all mortgage foreclosures, compared to 2 percent caused by death. (Health Affairs, *The Policy Journal of the Health Sphere*, 2 February 2005.)

- Half of all personal U.S. bankruptcies, affecting 2 million people annually, were attributable to illness or medical bills. (MarketWatch: Illness and Injury as Contributors to Bankruptcy, *Health Affairs* Web Exclusive, February 2, 2005.)

Recommendation: Find out more about disability insurance and how it can replace your income if you cannot work.

Personal Umbrella Liability Insurance

Five hundred thousand dollars! One million dollars! Five million! We live in what is sometimes referred to as a "litigious" society. No matter how careful you may be, there is always the possibility that you will be involved in a lawsuit. If you ever have the misfortune to be sued because of an auto, boating or other accident (even something as innocent as a neighbor's son falling out of a tree on your property), the numbers tend to get pretty big pretty fast. If they outstrip your homeowner's or vehicle's liability limits, you risk losing everything you own. That's why many people purchase personal umbrella liability insurance, coverage that offers large amounts of protection for a relatively small premium.

This supplemental coverage helps protect your assets if you are sued by providing insurance against liability costs above the maximum limits in your homeowner's, automobile, boat and recreational vehicle policies. It is generally sold in high-dollar amounts, often in $1 million units. Premiums may run as low as several hundred dollars per year for the first $1 million of coverage (depending on policy, state and other factors), with additional amounts costing significantly less.

Your umbrella policy provides excess coverage on top of that furnished by your other policies. Many policies offer:

- Catastrophic coverage involving automobiles, watercraft, recreational vehicles and personal liability protection worldwide.

- Coverage for non-owned vehicles and boats.

- Defense costs and other expenses not covered under your primary insurance.

$$$

Wealth Builder #27
Review Your Insurance

Do you have enough insurance ... and the right kind?
To find out, go to and complete the next exercise located in the *Back to Basics Book of Money Workbook*.

$$$

What's Next: You are mastering the art and science of balancing your spending, reducing your debt, and living on your income. This involves day-to-day money management. Now let's look to the future, putting your money to work making more money, while you get to sit back and watch it grow.

Next: Couple Money Skill #10 Put Your Money on the Payroll

$$$

Couple Money Skill #10

Put Your Money On The Payroll
(Learn How to Build Wealth!)

> *"Money is like a stringed instrument;*
> *he who does not know how to*
> *use it properly will hear only*
> *discordant music."*
>
> *—Kahil Gibran*

One of the things I've tried to drive home in this book is that interest rates on borrowed money can eat you alive. You know the drill: if you owe $1,000 and the annual interest rate is 15 percent, you will shell out $150 in a year for the privilege of having borrowed that money. Well, now it's time to turn the tables. You have learned in previous chapters that you do not have to live on borrowed money and pay interest month after month. Now let's learn how to become the one who earns interest rather than pays it.

When you save money and put it into a savings account or certificate of deposit, you are actually lending that money to the financial institution. If you buy a U.S. Savings Bond, you are lending your money to the federal government, and Uncle Sam agrees to pay you a certain percentage in return. They are now paying you interest!

It works a little differently if you buy mutual funds or stock in a specific company. When you do this, you are purchasing a small ownership share in the company – or a business that invests in numerous businesses, in the case with mutual funds – and you indirectly share in their profits and losses.

You have seen how to save for emergencies and major purchases. You have set up savings or checking accounts to segregate and store your money, where you will make deposits and withdrawals as part of your monthly spending plan. You may earn a few pennies in interest. However, the main purpose has been to allocate and set aside money to be used later for specific purposes.

Now it is time to talk about putting your money to work earning more money. We are going to discuss how to grow your money and build future dollars for long-term financial independence (what we used to call retirement), as well as to accumulate perhaps a college fund that will be available 15 or 18 years from now so that you can provide your children with debt-free college educations. You will learn how to create a partnership, with you and your money working toward a common goal.

$$$

The Two Ways to Make Money

There are ONLY two ways to make money ... all jokes aside about printing it in your basement or marrying rich or hitting it big in the lottery.

The first way is *people* at work – putting in an hour's work for an hour's pay. This is how most of us make money. Working up to 2,000 hours each year, we trade our time and our talents for our daily bread. *The problem:* there are only so many hours in a day. No matter what our income, it is difficult to become financially independent simply by working for a living. Fortunately, there is a second way to make money.

The second way is *money* at work. This involves putting a portion of our "earned" income to work in savings and investments to generate "unearned" income. Money making money! The concept is so simple it's almost frightening. That's how the rich get richer. But ANYBODY can do it. It's how you can help guarantee your own financial freedom, so you can live today and retire tomorrow on your own terms.

$$$

The Magic of Compound Interest

The money-at-work principle is simple: money begets money. A dollar saved can add up to a great deal more than a dollar earned. That's because, as long as you put it to work producing a respectable return, it will compound and grow. Given time, even a small amount of money can double, double and double again ... literally mushrooming as earnings compound and then compound again.

Here's an example of how it works. Imagine that you decide to save $1,000 a year for retirement. That breaks down to a little more than $83 a month, or roughly $20 a week ... the cost of a pizza with lots toppings. Now let's put that money to work making money for you rather than spending it on a pizza. Here is how this money can grow over time, based on several what-if rates of return.

Value of $1,000 Invested Annually at Three Interest Rates* (Interest Compounded Annually)						
Rate	10 Yrs.	15 Yrs.	20 Yrs.	25 Yrs.	30 Yrs.	40 Yrs.
2%	$10,950	$17,300	$24,300	$32,000	$40,600	$60,400
4%	$12,000	$20,000	$29,800	$41,600	$56,100	$95,000
6%	$13,200	$23,300	$36,800	$54,900	$79,100	$154,800
8%	$14,500	$27,200	$45,800	$73,100	$113,300	$259,900
10%	$15,900	$31,800	$57,300	$98,400	$164,500	$442,300

* Interest rates are presented to illustrate the effects of compounding. They do not represent the return of any particular investment. Results are rounded to the nearest $100.

Let's take a close look at that chart. Look how your money can grow over time. Even if you put it in a savings account earning a very modest 2 percent rate of return, it would grow to more than $60,000 over 40 years. Now keep in mind that $40,000 of that money came from your own deposits. Still, that leaves more than $20,000 your money earned while you just sat back and watched it grow. This is a long (and wonderful) way from the days of paying interest to borrow money from other people! It is also the steadiest, most reliable way to grow your money.

Three important points to keep in mind when it comes to putting your money to work:

1. **It takes discipline and commitment.** Based on the example above, the first step to earning money over the long term is to continue to put that money to work every month – month after month, year after year.

2. **It takes time to make it to the big bucks.** The serious compounding of interest takes place in the later years. That means you need to start early and contribute as long as you can. For example, at 6 percent, it takes 20 years for the money in our example to reach $36,800. Then over the next 20 years, it jumps to more than $154,000, or four times more.

3. **The average rate of return matters a lot.** Over 40 years, for example, the difference between a 4 percent return and an 8 percent return is not just double $95,000 (which would be $190,000). Instead, it comes to $259,900, or nearly $70,000 more than simply doubling the money.

Now imagine that you put aside $2,000 a year, or about $167 a month. In 25 years, if it earns an average rate of return of 6 percent, you will have nearly $110,000 waiting for you! That's one of the greatest non-secrets of how to build wealth over time: put your money to work for you making money! Save $4,000 a year, a little more than $333 a month, and you will have nearly $220,000 in 25 years. And then, if you decide to live off the interest on $220,000, based on a 6 percent return, you will receive $13,200 a year, $1,100 a month, and never touch the $220,000 principal. That's how people create financial independence.

Now, before you begin dreaming about putting your money to work generating double-digit earnings, keep in mind that it's easy to *talk* about raking in 4 percent, 6 percent, even 10 percent or higher returns. I remember back in the early 1980s when my money market account (and such accounts are historically known for earning moderately safe, fairly low returns) was cranking out 18 percent returns that I thought would never quit. They did! There was a time recently, however, when those rates dropped to below 1 percent. And then, of course, there is the real risk of losses that can result from some investments, such as stocks and mutual funds in a down economy.

Now, I am not an investment guru. I go to my guru for that advice. So, I will not tell you where to put your money or how to invest it. There is no skill and very little risk involved in putting your money into savings accounts, U. S. Savings Bonds, certificates of deposit and, to some degree, money market accounts that earn fairly modest returns. However, I caution that there is a lot to learn about moving to the deeper end of the pool, where the potential for larger returns exists. That is because, almost invariably, the larger the potential rewards, the greater the actual risks of loss. So, move forward with caution.

$$$

Getting Started Putting Your Money to Work

That caution having been offered, are you ready to start putting your money to work? Perhaps you are just starting to send money ahead. The idea is to get solid, competitive returns, but… I'll say it again: keep in mind that, in general, the higher the potential for return, the greater the risk. For instance, a savings account, fully insured and protected by the bank, will pay the lowest return on your money, but it will be guaranteed and very "liquid" (meaning you can access the money very easily). The goal is safety in exchange for a modest return. As the guarantees begin to drop off (if you get into mutual funds, stocks, real estate), the potential for reward may increase … but also will the potential for serious loss. I know some people who lost 50 percent of the value of their portfolios when the market took an ugly turn in 2000, and then again in 2008. One couple went from a comfortable net worth of $450,000 (excluding their home) down to under $250,000.

So, let's assume you are not a wildcat investor with a ten-gallon hat looking to double your dough on one high-risk roll of the dice. Also, if you are like most people, you may have neither the time nor the inclination to become a Wall Street Wizard. What you really want is enough information and knowledge to participate in key financial decisions and be able to talk to (and understand) your professional advisor.

Ten Recommendations

The primary reason people hesitate to become involved in investing is lack of financial education. Just remember that successful investing and financial management are learned skills that anyone can acquire. Still, there is a lot to learn, and you may decide, like the majority of people, that a little knowledge is all you need, and then rely on the expertise of professional financial advisers.

Here are ten recommendations to help you expand your financial knowledge:

1. **Raise your IQ (Investment Quotient).** Learn the basics. Attend investment seminars. Visit the library or surf the internet. Buy a book on the ABCs of investing. Start scanning the financial page of your local newspaper. (Other publications worth looking at are *The Wall Street Journal*, *Investors Business Daily*, and *Barron's Weekly*.) Take this self-education as far as you want.

2. **Seek good advice** from a professional who will walk you through the strange land of putting your money to work. Few investors go it alone. The right adviser serves as a guide, and is not only licensed and knowledgeable about

investments, but also skilled at helping clients understand their unique needs and make sound decisions. That is why it is crucial that you find someone who is knowledgeable, who you can trust and with whom you feel comfortable.

3. **Have objectives** that go beyond simply "make money." Work with your advisor to develop a plan, and then stick with it. This will involve mapping out your goals and identifying your risk tolerance. Determine what you want to accomplish, and what you are willing to do, investment wise, to achieve goals. In other words, develop a long-term strategy, a blueprint that reflects your long-term objectives.

4. **Stay within your comfort zone.** Never put money into an investment you do not understand or with which you are uncomfortable. If an "opportunity" looks intriguing, slow down and do your homework before you make any decisions. In other words, make sure your investments pass the "sleep test." If your investment keeps you tossing and turning at night, your money is in the wrong place.

5. **Avoid hot tips** from your rich Uncle Louie or your neighbor's barber. Effective investing is the result of a planned strategy based on your unique and individual objectives and situation.

6. **Invest for value and quality.** Unless you're a wild-catter who likes the thrill of big-time speculation, don't "play" with your money. Select quality investments that will help you meet your objectives. If you're looking for a thrill, buy lottery tickets or go scuba diving in shark-infested waters.

7. **Seek balance.** The adage about not putting all your eggs in one basket is sound advice. There's nothing wrong with certificates of deposit for short-term needs. Nor is there anything wrong with throwing some mad money into highly speculative penny stocks now and then. However,

it is often recommended that the majority of a person's money should be diversified among vehicles that reflect long-term objectives.

8. **Don't ignore the risks.** You can lose money if you fail to make knowledgeable, informed decisions. So, be sure you understand the potential risks before acting.

9. **Be disciplined. Be patient.** Forget about the overnight millionaire stuff. Successful investors generally are those who invest sometimes-small amounts regularly and systematically. They understand that their goals will not be achieved overnight. At the same time, they stay the course. Some people try to "read" the market and keep one step ahead of trends. The result is often confusion and anxiety over every market fluctuation and how they should react: "Should I buy or should I sell? Hibernate with the bears or run with the bulls? Move into bond funds, put more into stock funds, or go for safety in fixed-return vehicles?" Instead, if you and your advisor have done your homework, don't flinch in the face of downturns without strong evidence that a change of course is advisable.

10. **Review and adjust your strategy periodically** in light of changing economic conditions; your own personal life cycle changes, goals and financial situation; and new opportunities that may arise.

Bull markets. Bear markets. Any time can provide opportunities for people who understand their choices. No, we haven't discussed whether you should put your money into stocks, bonds, mutual funds or hog belly futures. Those decisions will come later, once you have a good grasp of investment basics and trusted advisor on tap.

$$$

145

$$$

Saving for Your Children's College Educations

When dealing with long-term goals, such as accumulating a substantial sum of money over time for your children's college educations, start with the amount you know you want to have available. Then calculate the number of years before you will need it. Finally, select an assumed interest rate. The chart on the next page makes it easy. Using the chart, look for the number of years to reach your goal and the rate of return you estimate you will earn as you save and invest the money earmarked for that goal. (When it comes to the rate of return, I recommend keeping it modest and realistic, perhaps as low as 4 percent.)

Using the chart, find the factor that rests at the intersection of the chosen rate of return and the number of years available to achieve the goal. Multiply the cost of the goal by this factor. The result is the amount that must be save each year to achieve the goal.

For example, if your goal is to have $25,000 for your child's education in 15 years, assuming a 4 percent rate of return, you will need to save $1,275.50 each year, or just over $100 a month. ($25,000 X .0499 = $1,247.50.) If the rate of return is 6 percent, you will need to save $1,075 a year, or just under $90 a month.

How Much Must You Save
Each Year to Reach Your Goal?

Yrs. to Goal	2%	4%	6%	8%	10%	12%	14%
1	0.9800	0.9600	0.9400	0.9200	0.9000	0.8800	0.8660
2	0.4950	0.4902	0.4854	0.4808	0.4762	0.4717	0.4673
3	0.3268	0.3203	0.3141	0.3080	0.3021	0.2963	0.2907
4	0.2426	0.2355	0.2286	0.2219	0.2155	0.2092	0.2032
5	0.1922	0.1846	0.1774	0.1705	0.1638	0.1574	0.1513
6	0.1585	0.1508	0.1434	0.1363	0.1296	0.1232	0.1172
7	0.1345	0.1266	0.1191	0.1121	0.1054	0.0991	0.0932
8	0.1165	0.1085	0.1010	0.0940	0.0874	0.0813	0.0756
9	0.1025	0.0945	0.0870	0.0800	0.0736	0.0677	0.0622
10	0.0913	0.0833	0.0759	0.0690	0.0627	0.0570	0.0517
11	0.0822	0.0741	0.0668	0.0600	0.0540	0.0484	0.0434
12	0.0746	0.0666	0.0593	0.0527	0.0468	0.0414	0.0367
13	0.0681	0.0601	0.0530	0.0465	0.0408	0.0357	0.0312
14	0.0626	0.0547	0.0476	0.0413	0.0357	0.0309	0.0266
15	0.0578	0.0499	0.0430	0.0368	0.0315	0.0268	0.0228
16	0.0536	0.0458	0.0390	0.0330	0.0278	0.0234	0.0196
17	0.0500	0.0422	0.0354	0.0296	0.0247	0.0205	0.0169
18	0.0467	0.0390	0.0324	0.0267	0.0219	0.0180	0.0146
19	0.0438	0.0361	0.0296	0.0241	0.0195	0.0158	0.0127
20	0.0412	0.0336	0.0272	0.0219	0.0175	0.0139	0.0110
21	0.0388	0.0313	0.0250	0.0198	0.0156	0.0122	0.0095
22	0.0366	0.0292	0.0230	0.0180	0.0140	0.0108	0.0083
23	0.0347	0.0273	0.0213	0.0164	0.0126	0.0096	0.0072
24	0.0328	0.0256	0.0197	0.0150	0.0113	0.0085	0.0063
25	0.0312	0.0240	0.0182	0.0137	0.0102	0.0075	0.0055

$$$

Saving for Retirement

Retirement saving poses a special problem for couples these days for several reasons:

1. We're retiring earlier than ever.

2. We're living longer than ever before.

3. Government plans (as in Social Security) are becoming unreliable.

4. Employer-sponsored pension plans are also becoming unreliable.

As a result, couples need to take more of the responsibility on themselves.   For example, imagine living to 100.   Imagine blowing out a hundred candles on that birthday cake. You just might.

You could be one of a growing number of centenarians in this country. In 2003, there were 60,000 men and women who had passed the century mark, reports the U.S. Census Bureau. By 2010, that number will break 129,000, and by 2050, the number of people in the U.S living to 100 will be nearly 850,000 — 14 times what it is today.[11]

Will you be one of them? You may be. In our society, we're pushing back the whole idea of old age. Most of us expect to live into our 70s and maybe our 80s.   Now, it's common for Americans to see their 90th or even 100th birthdays ... and to be in pretty good health for most of that time.

The point: the world has changed dramatically over the last 35 years. During the next 35 years, it is likely to keep changing, and at an even faster pace.

---

[11] "America's Future: Living to 100, Amid Abundant Diversity," The Nielsen Company, 2008.

One thing is certain. If you are still working, it is a good idea to build up your financial security nest egg. The goal is to empower yourself to live without financial worry in your senior years – no matter how long you live – and avoid becoming a burden on others.

Still, this is an issue that most people have not addressed, primarily because many Americans believed they were on track for a comfortable retirement, at least before the economic setbacks of 2008. Even now, too many people are not focusing on their retirement needs. As a result, they could be in for a terrible surprise in the future.

Some are counting on Social Security. However, they need to remember that Social Security was never intended to keep recipients in the lap of luxury, but only to provide a safety net. The average benefit for a retired worker (as of January 2009) was $1,153 a month, or just over $13,800 a year.[12]

Also let's say you have "enough" money, but enough for how long? There is a real danger of outliving your assets. For the sake of discussion, let's say that you have accumulated $300,000 by retirement. How long will it last? That depends on how much your nest egg earns and how much you withdraw each year.

Example: If the principal earns 7 percent on average, and you withdraw 8 percent of your initial principal, or $24,000, each year, your money will last 30 years. That *might* be adequate, but there are no guarantees, especially if you consider that life expectancies should continue to increase in the coming decades.

$$$

---

[12] "2009 Social Security Changes," Social Security Administration, January 2009.

$$$

Choosing the Right Saving Vehicles for Retirement

The benefit of saving for retirement is that you can put your money into a tax-advantaged account. I will not attempt to go through all the fine points of the various financial vehicles available. This is where the recommendation is to talk to an experienced financial representative. I will, however, summarize the concepts here briefly.

The Tax Value of Money

The federal government gets its pound of flesh in taxes on just about everything you earn, while the states slice off a few more ounces, as well. This can be frustrating when you're attempting to accumulate money for such long-term goals as retirement or your children's college educations ... or if you are simply looking for ways to maximize your net returns on money you put aside to build wealth.

Fortunately, taxes are not inevitable. In many cases, they can be deferred or completely avoided, all quite legally. The result could be thousands of dollars in income-tax savings to you each year. This is money that stays in your pocket, and that you can use to help you and your family achieve your financial objectives.

Tax basics: At the risk of over-simplification, from the point of view of the IRS, there are three different types of income:

1. **Taxable income.** For most of us, this is our earned income, what we receive from work. It also includes "unearned" income from investments, rental properties, and other unsheltered or nonqualified sources. Depending on your tax bracket, you could pay to Uncle Sam nearly 35 cents of every fully taxable dollar you earn. (Under current law, returns labeled as "capital gains" may be taxed at a lower rate.)

2. **Tax-deferred income,** also referred to as tax-sheltered income. Tax deferral means no tax is due in the current year in which it is earned. However, it generally will be taxable at a later date, when the funds are distributed or "constructively received" and available for your use, such as at retirement. As a rule, money that accumulates in a qualified retirement plan is tax-deferred. This can include interest, dividends and capital appreciation credited to IRAs, Simple Plans, Simplified Employee Pensions, Keogh Plans, 401(k) plans and other pension plans. The benefit is that it is possible to earn current rates of return and enjoy tax advantages.

3. **Tax-exempt income** is the third type of income. This money is never subject to federal tax (nor, in many cases, state tax). The best example is a Roth IRA. If you qualify, all earnings are tax-free, even when withdrawn. However, you cannot deduct your contributions.

Recommendation: Tax issues are just one aspect of selecting the best-choice financial vehicle for your needs and situation. Your choices should reflect your overall financial strategy and risk tolerance. That's why the best advice here is to talk to a financial professional.

$$$

Getting Professional Advice

Maybe you are not ready to begin an investment program. Perhaps you are still comfortable just putting your money into savings accounts and certificates of deposit. Nonetheless, you should begin looking at your prospects. The reason is simple. Over the last nine sections of this book, you have learned how to manage your money and begin putting it to work for you and your family. We have even discussed, in general terms, the idea of long-term goals and plans. Now it is time to bring it all together into a comprehensive, organized program.

Best of all, you do not have to go it alone. Oh, you certainly can if you want. However, there is a wealth of support available. Much of it is available at little or no charge. The two most logical places to start:

1. **Your financial institution.** Your bank or credit union is in the business of managing money. A personal banker or customer- service employee can usually give you direction and advice about how to save and grow your money.

2. **A financial representative.** These individuals go by a number of different names: insurance agent, insurance representative, financial planner, financial advisor, and so on. They are licensed professionals trained in helping their clients solve their financial problems and achieve their objectives. In addition to discussing insurance and investment products, they can help you set up college funding programs and retirement funds. Take advantage of these sources of advice and information.

Wealth Builder #30
Investing In Good Advice

The right professional is worth his or her weight in gold. To find a financial advisor that is right for you, go to and complete the next exercise located in the *Back to Basics Book of Money Workbook.*

$$$

What's Next: You are managing your money on a daily, weekly and monthly basis. You are whittling down your debt, and you are beginning to send long-term money ahead. You are probably already getting used to integrating your money management into your daily activities. You now know all you need to know to achieve financial stability. The final step is learning how to carry through with all you've learned each and every day.

Next: Live it Every Day

$$$

A Final Word

Live It Every Day
(Learn How to Transform 10 Skills into a
Lifetime of Financial Peace and Prosperity)

> *"Just do it!"*
>
> *—Nike Shoes*

By getting this far, you have devoted a great deal of time to straightening out your finances. You are to be congratulated. This means that you are doing more to manage your money than more than 95 percent of the people in this country. Now it is time to make money management a permanent, integrated part of your life and your lifestyle. In other words, live what you have learned every day. Make effective money management a habit that you practice every day. Do this, master this final money management skill, and the many benefits of financial security and peace will be yours for life.

Many people set out to take charge of their financial situations. It's sort of like quitting smoking. They are not always successful the first time, or even the second time they make the attempt. They can "fall off the wagon," as they say. You will have setbacks and days of frustration and disappointment. Do not be discouraged. The key is persistence.

$$$

Married Couples Have the Greatest Success

Remember, this book is for couples. It can work if you are financially committed in a mutual understanding. However, its real strength results from those who are married couple. The simple truth is that marriage and prosperity are closely linked. Not only do married people live longer and are healthier than

154

their single and even cohabiting counterparts, but they tend to be more financially stable and prosperous.

This is like a business partnership. Even with close friends, it takes that legal document to avoid misunderstandings. It's the same with other contracts. A handshake may work, but being able to go back and check the contract clauses when a dispute arises is always advisable.

Besides, cohabiting may work okay if you are financially broke. However, as you apply what you have learned in this book, your finances will begin to change. Add money into your relationship – become financially committed to each other – and the vague nature of cohabiting almost always leads to problems. So, you can do this if you are not married. However, there is a telltale lack of financial and legal commitment if you are merely cohabiting.

This is not meant to be a judgment on lifestyles – just a fact of life. Married couples tend to stick to it and tough it out better. Perhaps it is because they have more to gain by working together and more to lose by not doing so. If you are not married, yes, I understand that the divorce rate is high and the other arguments in favor of cohabiting. My only point is that married couples tend to be more financially stable.

But Divorce Is a Financial Killer

Now that I've preached about the financial value of marriage, I must point out that the most effective way to destroy finances is divorce. Divorce is not only expensive going in, but the negative impact can continue for years. Not only do money problems often lead to divorce, but divorce also leads to money problems, as assets are divided and destroyed.

In general, couples who remain married are financially better off over time than those who divorce.

Bob & Mary: Together for 35 Years

Bob and Mary have been married for 40 years. They started out with nothing but love for each other and dreams for the future. They never made a great deal of money. Neither was a professional. They were just hard-working folks.

They bought a home, raised three sons, two of whom went to college, saved their money, but also did without nothing. They both retired on their 40ᵗʰ wedding anniversary, financially secure for life.

Jerry & Judy & Jackie & Jana: Three Marriages and Counting

Then there was Jerry, who married Judy, his college sweetheart, at age 21. They both worked hard and built a prosperous lifestyle. By the time Jerry was 43, they had a nice home, three children, a cottage on a lake, a boat and three cars, and they traveled on nice vacations about three times a year. They were also building up retirement assets so they would be on target to retire to financial independence by age 60.

Unfortunately, they had everything but happiness, so after more than 20 years of marriage, they divorced. Everything was divided equally.

Then Jerry met Jackie shortly after his divorce from Judy. They moved in together. The relationship lasted five years, during which time Jerry's net worth declined.

Things didn't get any better over time. By the time he met and moved in with Jana when he was 54, his net worth had declined from a high of nearly $1 million while married to Judy to just over $200,000. Retirement would not be an option.

Marriage & Money

All the tongue-in-cheek debates about toilet seat positions and Mars vs. Venus aside, most married people enjoy traveling down the road of life as a couple. The stability and routine generally lead to prosperity and longevity. At the same time, it also brings with it financial responsibilities.

The U.S. Census Bureau reported that the average asset value owned by married couples is $223,194. For singles, it stands at half that ($111,951) for men; even less ($85,319) for women.[13] This is due in part to the dual incomes, but also to the ability to engage in long-range planning.

Here's a bonus: married people are also healthier. As one Associated Press headline put it, "Married people healthier than singles."[14] According to a study by the National Center for Health Statistics, in every age category, married men and women report fewer incidences of poor health. Between age 18 and 44, according to the study, only 4.5 percent of married people reported poor health. By contrast, 14.1 percent of widowed individuals and 10.6 percent of divorced or separated men and women rated their health as poor. The bottom line: married people are generally healthier and wealthier.

Learning to Live It Every Day

By now you are already enjoying many of the benefits of being in control of your finances. You have laid some incredible groundwork. Sure, you are probably pinching pennies in some areas, but that means you are making those important and sometimes tough decisions. Plus, remember, you are in this for the long haul. Every day, month and year, the process will get easier and bear increasingly abundant rewards in terms of financial stability and personal satisfaction. You see, that is one of the best parts: a stable relationship and stable finances are

---

[13] "Asset Ownership of Households: 2000," U.S. Census Bureau (www.census.gov)
[14] Associated Press, December 16, 2004.

interconnected. Best of all, taking this ongoing step together is fairly easy.

Wealth Builder #31
Creating a Life Plan of Financial Prosperity

It's time to develop your ongoing strategy for building and expanding your financial security. Go to and begin the final exercise located in the *Back to Basics Book of Money Workbook*.

Congratulations!

Well, you did it. Congratulations! Do not take your accomplishment lightly. You have put in a lot of time and effort. Yes, it took some work, and you are not done yet. However, the payoff should already be underway, and it will just keep getting better each month and year.

For more ideas and to receive a free weekly newsletter with tips and ideas, visit www.b2bbookofmoney. It includes daily money management tips and ideas to help you live increasingly more successfully and prosperously on your money.